SHELLEY'S STUDY GUIDES
EDITED BY WALTER HARDING

Maggie, The Red Badge of Courage
Selected Short Stories and
Representative Poems
A Study Guide

STEPHEN CRANE, on a cardboard rock in a photographer's studio, poses in outfit he wore as war correspondent for the New York *World* and *Journal*.

Stephen Crane

(Copyrighted by Florence Coughlin, daughter of William Crane)

Stephen Crane's

MAGGIE
THE RED BADGE
OF COURAGE

SELECTED SHORT STORIES

REPRESENTATIVE POEMS

A STUDY GUIDE
by Hans Gottschalk

SHELLEY PUBLISHING COMPANY
Bound Brook, New Jersey

Contents

Preface

THIS Guide uses one of the oldest pedagogical approaches known to man, the method of self-questioning. Through answering questions chronologically regarding what is happening to whom why and with what consequences should prompt a more thorough understanding of a literary work. Once analysis is complete, synthesis must be reinvoked, so that the work will reassert its totality in our consciousness, a totality made subconsciously clearer, fuller and richer by details the analysis has furnished.

The purpose of this particular guide extends beyond a single work. It considers two novels, a novelette, a number of short stories and several poems by Stephen Crane, roughly in the order of their writing (the revised rather than the first edition of *Maggie* is used). In the process, each work should yield its own patterns of characterization, imagery and outlook. The several works ought in turn reveal parallels and differences from one another. Finally, the cumulative study should lead to the recognition of cumulative patterns in the overall picture. And we can remind ourselves that beyond Crane are other authors and their works, to be read just as carefully, intensively and interpretively.

Hopefully, the method is self-inducing as well as self-questioning.

The vocabulary items at chapter ends, never extensive for one who emphasizes direct experience as Crane does, diminishes to the near-vanishing point for obvious reasons. Research questions are designed to illuminate specific works, to take in related works not included in the question guide, and generally to build an awareness and understanding of the total Stephen Crane.

The critical excerpts begin with a general one on Crane's naturalism, continue with more specific ones chronologically discussed, and concluding with some overall comments.

Maggie, The Red Badge of Courage
Selected Short Stories and
Representative Poems
A Study Guide

Stephen Crane (1871-1900)

Crane was descended on his father's side from a line of early New Jersey settlers who had distinguished themselves in war and politics. The father himself was a Methodist minister, converted from Presbyterianism on the question of infant damnation, who always overworked and was always underpaid, and so with difficulty supported his large family. He had established himself as an author of clerical repute: *The Arts of Intoxication*—tobacco, opium and alcohol, and *The Popular Amusements*—baseball, the stage, novels. Crane's mother derived from a line of Pennsylvania Methodist clergymen. Both parents were earnest but very kind and forgiving, as witness the mother taking in a young unmarried mother-to-be.

From these sources may well have stemmed Crane's own inclination toward an aristocracy of worth and principle in the Cooper pattern, with a strong democratic affinity for the underdog. Again, he was to try all the devil's works against which his father had inveighed, but in a deliberate quest for experience rather than in revolt against parental edict. Perhaps that is why his indulgences remained moderate, contrary to the general gossip that had him enslaved to them.

His father died when Crane was eight, the mother continuing in churchwork for both income and outlet. Stephen himself early knew repeated illness, even while the instance of his father uncomplainingly working himself to death was still a vivid family memory. With his mother often away on speaking trips, Stephen became the special care of sister Agnes, fifteen years his senior and a teacher, who encouraged him in his earliest writing. Unfortunately, her salutary influence was removed by her early death. One wonders, whether the female pattern of household authority prompted Crane's later inclination to older women.

Crane's formal schooling was limited to two and a half years at a private secondary institute and a semester each at Lafayette College and Syracuse University. At the former he shared 'the vivid Civil War experience of table head, Rev. General John B. Van Petten. At both the latter he paid far more mind to baseball than to studies, hoping to become a professional player, despite being in pain with almost every throw.

Crane's lack of interest in learning extended to literature as well. Crane read little, in part at least because he felt that he must live with no time lost since so little time remained (he usually, it turns out optimistically, set his life span at 35 years). Thus he became an arch example of the American experiential tradition; he sensed, he felt, he acted primarily at the subconscious level. He becomes another incarnation of Cooper's raw American innocent, the city and its vices notwithstanding.

One other interest claimed his time—writing. At Syracuse he wrote the first version of *Maggie* in a matter of days. Already his work pattern was emerging: slow incubation, writing at white heat, then laborious polishing, shaping, revising. Thus after he moved to New York, spring 1891, he did two more versions; even then he was not satisfied, and radically revised it for its second edition (1896). Meanwhile, finding no publisher for the novel, Crane had it printed early in 1893 at his own expense under the pseudonym "Johnston Smith," later using most of the 1100 copies for firewood. There is a touch of Cranean irony in his own unknowing contribution to its later collectors value of over $3000 a copy.

Aside from writing *Maggie*, Crane was a correspondent for the *New York Tribune*. To it he contributed most of what are now called the "Sullivan County Sketches." He also did a series on Asbury Park where his bent for irony backfired. Reviewing a parade of the Junior Order of United American Mechanics, he let his irony play over walkers and watchers alike, displeasing everybody. Since the *Tribune's* editor was running for the Vice-Presidency, Crane and his brother Townley, the actual head of the Asbury bureau, were fired. Townley was later reinstated, but thereafter the *Tribune's* reviews of Stephen's writings were something less than cordial.

Romance had been part of Crane's life throughout.

Redheaded Harriet Mattison, who died shortly; a girl from Sioux City; Jenny Pierce—schoolday crushes. Then began his association with older women—Helen Trent, social and betrothed; Lily Brandon Munroe, young matron later divorced, a source of strength during the difficult days of gaining recognition. It was for her that he summarized the artistic credo toward which he had been deliberately moving:

"To speak, to tell you of my success, dear, is rather more difficult. My career has been more of a battle than a journey. You know, when I left you, I renounced the clever school in literature. It seemed to me that there must be something more in life than to sit and cudgel one's brains for clever and witty expedients. So I developed all alone a little creed of art which I thought was a good one. Later I discovered that my creed was identical with the one of Howells and Garland and in this way I became involved in the beautiful war between those who say that art is man's substitute for nature and we are the most successful in art when we approach the nearest to nature and truth, and those who say—well, I don't know what they say. They don't, they can't say much but they fight villianously [*sic*] and keep Garland and I out of the big magazines. Howells, of course, is too powerful for them.

If I had kept to my clever, Rudyard-Kipling style, the road might have been shorter but, ah, it wouldn't be the true road. The two years of fighting have been well-spent. And now I am almost at the end of it. This winter fixes me firmly. . . . ." (*Letters*, 31-32)

Crane was generally somewhat ill at ease in women's social company. He evidently needed the reassurance of more mature women who could guide both him and his affairs. More importantly to readers of Crane, here lies probably a strong reason for the comparatively few women in his fiction, and for the uncomplicated nature of those that do appear compared to that of his men.

Recognition came to Crane first from reigning realists of the day—younger Hamlin Garland, established William Dean Howells, and others. Their encouragement confirmed Crane in his work on *The Red Badge of Courage*, already in progress. Again there was the period of inner readying, including the reading of borrowed books on the Civil War (of little or no help), the concentrated write-through in extraordinary short order, the careful fashioning of the finished piece.

In the fall of 1893 he had also come to the writing of poetry. It came to him readily and in nearly final form. He exulted in it and in the ease of its utterance, but curiously the fountain seems to have gushed only during two brief intervals of his life. This first one resulted in the volume *The Black Riders and Other Lines* (1895), the latter his term for his poems. Copland and Day took the poems under option, but wished to delete many as unfit. Crane says they would take the anarchy right out of the book and with it "all the ethical sense" (*Letters*, p. 40), especially since they would remove all those that speak of God.

Early in 1894 Crane had to borrow $30 from Garland to get back his typewriter which he had given as security for the cost of having *The Red Badge of Courage* typed. He continued to refine, the whole compositional period was about a year, and read proofs of it during a western tour on which he had been sent by the Irving Bacheller syndicate.

Late in 1893 a considerably shortened version had appeared in certain syndicated papers, including *The Nebraska State Journal*, where Willa Cather read it in proof. When he stopped by on his western jaunt, she bided her time and one evening got from him a long self-revealing talk, in which she found him more bitter than anyone she ever knew, then or later. This opinion underscores his empathy for the victims of tenements and war, reflects directly the naturalistic outlook of the poems just then achieving publication, and parallels the savage irony already at the heart of all he wrote.

Crane's 1895 trip, brief as it was, furnished material for a whole series of stories—western, southwestern, Mexican—written during his remaining years. It also continued the duality of his writing mentioned to Willa Cather—immediate press dispatches and sketches for money, and artistic pieces for keeps. Curiously, his point of view in the two categories, perhaps in part because of his ironical approach, developed in paradoxical fashion with "I" narration increasingly dominant in supposedly objective news dispatches, and third person continuing as standard in fiction and verse.

The year 1896 saw Crane attain popular as well as critical success, one primarily attributable to the smash reviews of the English edition of *The Red Badge*. The reviews led to a re-evaluation of Crane's work here and to thirteen editions during the year. The revised *Maggie* appeared and also got a substantial boost in sales. Crane had removed "a goodly number of damns" (*Letters*, p. 112), and raised Maggie's final solicitory attempts to an implicit and even pass-by level, thus strengthening the reader's sympathy for her.

Late in the year (1896) Crane was sent to cover the Cuban rebellion for the Bacheller syndicate. He never got to Cuba, but the trip brought irrevocable consequences. First, while awaiting passage in Jacksonville he met Cora Stewart who was to share most of the remainder of his brief life (there had also been older women—Nellie Crouse, Akron, and Amy Leslie, Chicago). Second, the ship in which he booked passage sank and he was one of several who survived. His dispatch on the disaster was followed by the fictional rendering of his own rescue, "The Open Boat," one of his finest stories.

Unable to reach Cuba, he went to Greece to cover the impending struggle between her and Turkey. Cora also went as correspondent under the alias Imogene Carter. This war lasted only a month, but the trip furnished material for a later novel and a short story. Also, Crane had brief experience under fire, Fleming's author testing himself. A second consequence was the common law marriage of Cora and Crane, her husband refusing a divorce. They settled in Oxted, Surrey, in a country house near Harold Frederic, Joseph Conrad, Edward and Constance Garnett, and later, at Brede Place, also Ford Madox Ford and Henry James.

The stay in England was prophetic of the final one: the Crane house became a stopping off place for friends, their friends, writers, ordinary American tourists. Often whole groups would come for days at a time. Cora coped with them as she could, feeding them too well to encourage departure. The drain on finances was matched only by the drain on Crane's creative time, later to be virtually catastrophic. On at least one occasion Crane left the house for some days to work. Crane kicked, but he also rather enjoyed playing lord of the manor. Moreover, he had learned that the short story and brief novel were his proper media, and these lent themselves to both his method of composition and the domestic situation. Thus despite the turmoil, a bad case of nerves, and verging constantly on painful illness, he managed to complete "The Monster," "The Bride Came to Yellow Sky," "Death and the Child," and "The Blue Hotel."

The sinking of the *Maine* on February 15, 1898, seemed to vex others more than Crane. Yet before long he was once more off to cover another war, the professional correspondent fulfilling the image (though first he tried to enlist), and yet also to satisfy once and for all the soldier in him.

In Cuba he was ill most of the time, several times suffering hallucinations. At least three times he deliberately stood up to draw enemy fire. He was snapped out of what, according to testimony, were trances and remained unwounded. Once he filed a story for a wounded correspondent and ran five miles each way for help. Suffering from fever and exhaustion he was put to bed, only to leave for the Puerto Rico campaign.

Afterward he holed up in Cuba, first at a hotel then at a boarding house, writing as though his life depended upon it. He finished his Greek novel *Active Service*, "The Price of the Harness," the poems "Intrigues," and, in fact, story after story and sketch after sketch, each sent to his agent with urgent pleas for money. Thus far biography is mute on why such desperate need for it, as meanwhile he did not even write to Cora, despite his being thought lost and she appealing to the Secretary of War for help in locating him.

After some weeks Crane went to New York and did the town, eventually cabling Cora that he was returning. She had taken in Kate Frederic and her three children after Frederic died, and was desperately trying to stay solvent against summonses and the loss of Ravensbrook. She was granted a lease at nominal rent of Brede Place. And there they all settled after Crane's homecoming.

There followed another hectic round of living like that before the Cuban interruption. Crane was, however, the worse for campaign wear. He worked, and desperately, at a series on famous battles, on war stories and memories, on Whilomville tales, on English sketches, on an Irish romance. He wrote against debts and pain and time, while Cora typed, proofread, corresponded. Both importuned incessantly for immediate moneys, to assure "Stephen" leisure to "show the world a book that will live," as Cora wrote (*Letters*, p. 203). And thus Crane spent his creative strength in a vain effort to keep all heads above water. This was likely to be impossible on any account, since Crane still tended to be "Baron of Brede."

Once more Crane thought of war as an escape from immediate pressures, this time in the Transvaal. But he was dissuaded, perhaps as much by his health, of which he knew considerably more than those about him, as by the requests of Cora, friends and publishers. Two trips followed, one to Paris, as he took his niece Helen to a school in Lausanne; the other to Ireland in quest of local color for *The O'Ruddy*.

The year wound up in a blaze of glory and the incurable wound. Crane, James, AEW Mason, Wells, Gissing and others collaborated on a seasonal play about the Ghost of Brede Place to be presented at the village schoolhouse. It was; and great gaiety reigned throughout the holidays, including a game, invented by H. G. Wells, for racing across the great smooth floors on broomsticks. At the end of the festivities Crane hemorrhaged and Wells had to cycle for a doctor. Thereafter Crane's doom was keenly evident. A desperation trip to the Black Forest—he was seen off at Dover by Conrad and others—meant only his dying elsewhere at Badenweiler instead of home at Brede. Robert Barr, entrusted at Dover in whispers about how to finish *The O'Ruddy*, quotes Crane as clearly sensing his end (*Letters*, 203): "Robert, when you come to the hedge—that we must all go over—it isn't bad. You feel sleepy—and—you don't care. Just a little dreamy curiosity—which world you're really in—that's all."

Maggie

1.

The first three chapters picture typical family and tenement life in Rum Alley during the childhood of Maggie and Jimmie.

1. Are we to consider the savage gang fight of the boys a usual occurrence? How do you know?

2. Why does Pete interfere in the fight?

3. Do the names of the sections represented by the two groups suggest anything about the neighborhood?

4. How can you ascertain whether the dialogue is authentic?

5. Why, do you think, does Crane not give the actual curses of the fighters?

6. What details cumulatively etch in the story's setting and mood?

7. Why do you think the author finds it necessary to say, "The two little boys, fighting in the modes of four thousand years ago, . . . ? Does this also apply to older boy Pete? See if it will apply to the approaching father and other grown-ups as well.

8. Are the father's actions and words in keeping with the fight? why or why not?

precipitately, catapultian power

2.

1. What do you think is meant by the expression "in curious postures of submission to something"?
Research Question:
Read T.S. Eliot's early poems "Four Preludes" and "Rhapsody on a Windy Night." Remembering that these were written a quarter century after Crane's story, what elements do you find that all three have in common? In what significant respects do they differ?

2. Why does Jimmie keep pummeling his sister Maggie? Maggie here both upbraids and curses Jimmie; and she had jerked Tommie along the street . . . What do these actions tell about her?

3. What is the significance of his father's dictum, "Leave yer sister alone on the street"?

4. Why is it important that the father "rushed from the room"? that the mother had a weeping spell as well as fighting ones?

5. Why is Jimmie described as "shrieking like a monk in an earthquake"?

6. Why should Jimmie be afraid of his mother, but not of his father or of other fellows? Why should he, of all of them, take refuge with the old woman downstairs?

7. What part does Tommie play in all the scuffling? Does this at all parallel Jimmie's struggles in his gang and with other gangs?

8. What does the old woman's last question suggest about the parental relationship of the family?

disdainfully, lamentations, quaveringly, rampant, contortions, imperturbably, prodigious

3.

1. Of what is Fifth Avenue—where the old woman from below goes to beg—here the symbol?

2. What is insinuated by the remark that the pennies were "contributed for the most part, by persons who did not make their homes in that vicinity"? Does this suggest any attitude on the part of Crane?

3. Why are the old woman's daily pursuits included at all, including her battling a young policeman?

4. Why should Jimmie be concerned about the unfairness of his father's drinking of the old woman's beer?

5. What is the function of alcohol for these people? Is the reader meant to relate the quantity and kind of drinking to their situation? Give reasons for your answer.

6. Why have we not heard the family's last name before, and hear it now dropped casually by neighbors listening to the parents battle?

7. Again, why is Jimmie so afraid of his mother —her grim, crimson face and closed eyes?

8. How would a Chopin nocturne go with the scene at the end of the chapter? Does Crane parallel exterior and interior description here?

9. How would you characterize the life pictured in the first three chapters? Are we to remember now the little boys battling?

Research question:

After the appearance of Darwin's *Origin of Species*, 1859, its central notions spread through the natural and then through the social sciences. One of these was natural selection, or the survival of the fittest. Does it seem to be part of this story, either directly or incidentally? Look up the background suggested before giving your carefully reasoned answer.

fervency, floundered, grovelled, strangulation

4.

Chapters 4, 5 and 6 describe the life of the grown-up Jimmie and Maggie (both Tommie and father have succumbed to the rigors of Rum Alley). They also offer Pete as contrast to that life.

1. Can you discover any reason why Tommie should survive so briefly and the father as long as he did?

Research Question:

In a history of New York City look up the nature and function of fire fighting companies in New York City in the late 19th century. Do you find any reasons for Jimmie's fear?

2. Why did the mission preachers make no impression on Jimmie and his cohorts? Why does Crane have them confuse the preacher with Christ, do you

suppose? What is the import of the preacher not understanding the question why he did not say "we" instead of "you"?

3. Why would Jimmie despise well-clothed people?

4. Does this edition of Jimmie fit the earlier one? List the details and extent of the consistency.

5. Is the statement "He was afraid of nothing" true? Does your answer suggest a parallel to his youth?

6. Do you think Jimmie was a good employee for his trucking concern? Why or why not?

7. Do you think that we are meant to take as truth the complaint of two women with infants that he was the father who ought to marry and support them and their children?

8. What does the last sentence add to the characterization of Jimmie? And why would he still be called Jimmie instead of Jim?

exhorter, raiment, malignant, despicable, opprobrium

5.

1. Maggie is here pictured as an exception. Has her youth pointed toward such? Is it plausible that such an exception as she survive?

2. How do you interpret "Twenty girls of various shades of yellow discontent"? Look up "synesthesia" in a glossary of literary terms or in your dictionary. Does the term apply here? Why or why not?

3. Why does Crane conclude the first paragraph with "At night she returned home to her mother"? Are we to take this sentence literally, figuratively or both?

Research Question:

Compare these experiences of Maggie and Jimmie with those of Huck Finn and his pappy in the earlier chapters of *Huck Finn*. Was pappy always this way? Another clue would be in *Tom Sawyer*. Do you suppose Mary Johnson was always as she is now?

4. How do you maintain order in the saloon trade, according to Pete? Is it similar to Jimmie's trucking world?

5. Pete is described as having "waved his hands like a man of the world who dismisses religion and philosophy, and says 'Rats!' " In the previous chapter Jimmie "became so sharp he believed in nothing." Can one really believe in nothing? What did the two really believe in?

6. Was it natural for Maggie to dream of an ideal lover? Why should she think Pete was that "ideal man"? Does her feeling fit the author's statement that opens the chapter?

gamin, dishevelled, Williamsburg, "dukes," "outa sight"

6.

1. What does Pete mean when he says one of his opponents "scrapped like a dago"? Does this suggest

that even intolerance and prejudice is governed by what the Petes and Jimmies value most? Why? Can we generalize their central value into that of this whole environment?

2. Maggie watches Pete's departure from the window. Is it she who thinks the following? "Here was one who had contempt for brass-clothed power; one whose knuckles could ring defiantly against the granite law. He was a knight." If so, where does she get the vocabulary? If not, why does the author not more clearly separate her action from this comment? Can the answer perhaps be both yes and no?

3. Analyze the chapter generally for the extent to which the author's point of view is within and outside of Maggie.

4. Why does Crane so carefully build up Maggie's imaginary picture of Pete's world concurrently with the messiness of her home life, particularly on the Friday for which Pete had made a date with her?

pinnacle, cretonne, lambrequin, prodigious, be-
draggled

7.

Chapters 7—13 show the romance and life of Pete and Maggie, when they go out together and after she has been deliberately ordered from the house by her mother. The reaction of Jimmie is typical of the brother who feels he must uphold the honor of his sister by beating up Pete.

1. Are we to take the comments on Pete's conduct as cultured and considerate straight, ironically, or both? Explain.

2. Why does Crane describe the whole show?

3. What is the contrast implied in the terms "the Bowery public" and the "theatre-going public"?

4. Why are American and Irish freedom and the star spangled banner made the climax of the show? Do you think Crane is satirizing the scene? Does he exhibit any sympathy?

5. What do Maggie's refusal of a kiss and Pete's concluding remark to himself seem to suggest about their future relationship? Are both reactions characteristic?

Research Question:

Look up the continuity of the American entertainment scene through the beer hall, music hall, cabaret, revue, vaudeville and night club. What elements tend to change? What characteristics remain relatively constant?

chandelier, condescension, "duffer"

8.

1. Do you think the women in Maggie's place of work look as they do only to her? Give reason(s) for your answer.

2. Can you interpret the nationality background of the boss from the brief bit of his dialect quoted?

3. Do you think Crane is anti-Jewish in speaking

of the pawnshops ("three gilt balls") to which Maggie's mother resorted as "where Hebrews chained them [the household articles] with chains of interest"?

4. The mother (do you think her name Mary is an intentional irony?) strikes out physically against the world which has treated her badly. Is this true of any of the others? What do those do, like Maggie, who cannot smash at the world physically?

5. Against what, do you think, does Crane want the reader to feel they are rebelling and revenging themselves? Would you call their reactions blind or not? Indicate reasons. May we be touching an underlying point of view here?

6. Why was Pete so fascinated by one small monkey at the zoo? Does the parallel go beyond what Pete himself sees?

7. Why did "Maggie and the rest of the audience" think that the melodramas were "transcendental realism"?

8. Problem for looking up: Some decades later O'Neill in "Anna Christie" had his waterfront characters acting big scenes in terms of the melodramas they went to see. Why did this not "come off"?

9. Do we have any equivalents of those melodramas, in which everything and everybody are good or bad, with hardly any in between? And even the bad in the audience cheer the good on stage?

10. Does Crane imply in the concluding sentence that everybody has his "as ifs," situations he experi-

ences vicariously which he hopes he could actually function in successfully?

fastidious, maledictions, confounded

9.

1. Why do you think Jimmie was so insistent upon getting his mother into their apartment?

2. Why could Jimmie not subdue his mother more easily, considering she was so much older and drunk as well?

3. What do your answers to questions 1 and 2 indicate about Jimmie's character?

4. Does Jimmie's victory over her make his mother feel humiliated and resentful, do you suppose? Does the appearance of Pete at this point help you answer the question?

5. The mother accuses Maggie of having "gone t'd' devil." Has she? If so, why doesn't Maggie show shame or at least admission? If not, why does Pete continue to court her all this time?

6. The chapter concludes with another of Crane's pithy understatements: "Maggie went." From previous experience with the technique, how would you interpret this sentence, even without reading further?

10.

1. Why does Jimmie so readily believe the woman downstairs about Maggie?

2. Why does the mother take the news so melo-dramatically?

3. Is Jimmie right, was (notice the tense) Maggie different? Does this, again, go beyond Jimmie's own interpretation?

4. Do the mother's melodramatics and Jimmie's re-solve to beat up the guilty man (Pete) show any ad-herence to a standard of morality? Explain.

5. Why are the tenement women so down on Mag-gie?

6. What is the double standard of morality fre-quently spoken of? Is it applicable to the present situ-ation?

Research Question:

In the opening scene of Hawthorne's *The Scarlet Letter* it is also the women who are hardest on the girl. Compare the two scenes to see whether the moti-vation is the same for the two groups of women.

11.

1. What does the opening sentence contribute to our earlier question regarding the function of alcohol in the book?

2. Why should the bar be so minutely described?

3. Why does the meeting of Jimmie, his companion and Pete seem like old home week?

4. Jimmie is described in "wild animal" terms; Pete has "the glare of a panther." And "the bravery of bulldogs sat upon the faces of the men." Do these,

together with earlier reference to the monkey, suggest an aspect of human behavior and the author's attitude toward it? Could Darwin, twice removed into social darwinism and into art, be invoked here?

5. Pete "shot a lurid glance at Jimmie." What color is suggested in the preferred meaning "lurid"? What other applications of the color have you noted, in retrospect? Images repeated so frequently usually embody a symbolical function. What do you think the repeated use of this color symbolizes in the book?

6. Once the fighting is under way, the intent of each is characterized: Pete "like the desire to kill;" Billie "like a wounded maniac;" and Jimmy "with the face of a sacrificial priest." How do you interpret these?

7. The "maniac" aspect soon grips all three in a "frenzy of blood." Note also the frenzies of the novel's opening fights, and those of mutual familial devotedness. If we remind ourselves that these men are still acting like the "little boys" of yore, we have three sets of images to characterize these men in the fight. What do all three have in common?

8. Do you find it in character that Jimmie should have an "ally" and so make the fight unfairly one-sided? Why do you think Crane uses that particular term several times?

9. At chapter's end Jimmie's "Ah, what's d' use?" echoes friend Billie's remark at the end of the previous chapter. Why the parallel?

10. What is the significance of Pete's "Don' make

no trouble" repeated here from earlier uses? How does it fit into the "what's d' use" parallel?

opulence, pyrotechnically

12.

1. Pete's demeanor in the beer hall is portrayed here as almost the duplicate of that in Chapter 7. Compare the tone of the two for any possible change.

2. Then Maggie was in Rum Alley with Pete's world beyond it; now she is in the latter, remembering and telling of her Rum Alley life. Does this suggest the present always requires a comparison and is therefore lived only in terms of past or future?

3. Maggie "did not feel like a bad woman." This suggests she too thinks of herself as "different," a fact borne out by her exit past the two painted women. Are we readers meant to agree with her? Are we meant to go also beyond her interpretation of "different" as we were meant to go beyond Jimmie's?

4. Why did the men, whose admiring glances at her Pete reveled in, make Maggie fear?

13.

1. Are we to accept the mother's lamentation regarding Maggie's conduct at face value or as a cover-up for guilt on her part? How do you know?

2. Why does Jimmie suggest bringing Maggie back home?

3. How does the mother's "She kin cry 'er two eyes out on deh stones of deh street" go with her "May Heaven forgive her"? What irony lies in the mother saying both?

4. Why, ironically, did Maggie "go t' d' devil"?

5. Why is Jimmie here, as on several previous occasions, made to have some qualms of conscience, whereas the mother seems to have none? How do their reactions affect the reader's attitude toward Maggie?

14.

The remaining chapters mirror Maggie's rejection, successively, by Pete; by her mother, Jimmie and the neighbors; by a clergyman; and by men and mankind in general. The rejections culminate in her walk to her death in the river. She is then taken back by family and neighbors as object for mourning and melodramatic forgiveness.

1. What is different about the atmosphere of this "hall" from those Pete and Maggie had been to before? Does it represent any change in Pete's attitude toward Maggie?

2. Interpret: Maggie: Pete=Pete: Nell

3. How do Freddie and the man from Buffalo fit into this proportion formula?

4. What do the language and dress of Nell and Freddie suggest about them?

5. What is the irony of Maggie's answer to Freddie's proposition, "I'm going home"?

6. Why is Freddie always referred to as "the mere boy"? Does this too have meaning in a double sense?

15.

1. What does Hattie's rejection by Jimmie prove about him?

2. Why should Maggie appeal beyond her mother to Jimmie? Is his answer characteristic? Explain.

3. Why should the very same old woman who gleefully told Jimmie the news in the first place now offer to take Maggie in, saying, "I aint got no moral standin' "?

16.

1. Pete's feeling regarding Maggie parallels that of Jimmie toward Hattie, note even the same "yehs told me—" uttered by both women. Why does Crane make the parallel so pronounced?

2. When Jimmie had become head of the family he had given Maggie two alternatives. What were they (Chapter 5)? What single alternative does Pete leave her with his remark, "Oh, go to hell!"?

3. A clergyman also rejects Maggie. Do you think he thinks she's about to make him a proposition?

4. Throughout the story there have been religious allusions: Devil's Row; go t' d' devil; confusing mis-

sion preacher and Christ; Jimmie's fighting "like a sacrificial priest;" two references to monks, one to Providence; a rejection by a clergyman. What do all these add up to in essential point of view or attitude of the narrator-author?

Research Question:

Could Crane's own family background have anything to do with this attitude?

17.

1. What contrast is set up at the beginning of the chapter before the "girl of the painted cohorts of the city" is introduced?

2. What do her glances and her attire testify about her?

3. Why was she once accosted as "old lady" and another time rejected as being "neither new, Parisian nor theatrical"?

4. Of what is Maggie finally the victim? Why? Why didn't she go back to the factory instead of becoming a girl of the streets? Did she really go to the devil, in author Crane's eyes, do you think? Give reasons for your answer.

18.

1. The second last man Maggie passed on her way to the river was "a man with blotched features." The end of this chapter finds Pete passed out on the floor,

with wine from an overturned glass dripping upon the blotches on the man's neck. What do these two references together suggest?

2. Why, do you think, it is "the man's" instead of "Pete's" neck?

3. Why does Maggie fail and why do the Nells, Mary Johnsons, and Jimmies survive? Will Pete survive? Give reasons for your answer.

19.

1. Why are chapters 18 and 19 added to a story called *Maggie* when Maggie is already dead?

2. Why is Jimmie pictured as soiled and unshaven when he enters?

3. What is the importance of the stress on judgment here, God's and Mary's?

4. Is Mary's scream of pain real or phony? Of what significance is the answer to this question as far as this chapter and the entire story is concerned?

Research Questions:

In Bret Harte's famous short story "The Luck of Roaring Camp" Kentuck remarks about his finger after he had seen Cherokee Sal's baby, "Rastled with it,—the d—d little cuss." Compare this and Kentuck's final remark from the point of sincerity with Mary Johnson's remarks about Maggie's baby shoes. Are both persons sincere? Is the sincerity of the respective writers the same?

Read Theodore Dreiser's short story, "The Sanctuary." Why does Dreiser's retelling of our story end differently? Is Dreiser making a point wholly different from Crane's or are the two essentially of the same view?

Crane wrote a story based on his own experience sleeping in a Bowery flophouse, "An Experiment in Misery." Analyze the feeling of the young protagonist the next day as, seated on a park bench, he views the city's buildings and bustle from a new point of view. How does it compare with the irony of Crane's point of view in *Maggie?*

Compare the first edition (it is actually the 4th draft) of *Maggie* with the first revised edition of 1896, the one used for this guide. What significant changes are there, especially in the ending of Chapter 17?

Another of Crane's Bowery sketches is "The Men in the Storm." Analyze how the frustration of the men, waiting in blizzard and late afternoon cold, expresses itself here also in physical force and how that force is dissipated by the opening of "the charitable house."

Still another of Crane's city stories is "A Dark-Brown Dog." What does the dog bring into the life of the child? How does even the dog become victim of the tenement environment? Compare the narration of this story with that of *Maggie*. What is the basic difference in approaches? Which is the more effective one? Why?

Did Crane perhaps deliberately take over the melodrama and put into it all the very environmental pressures and ironies that subconsciously drove the characters themselves to the melodrama?

Much speculation has centered about the influence of Zola's *L'Assommoir* on Crane, particularly in *Maggie*. Crane repeatedly called Zola dull, probably because Zola's detailing was primarily exterior, photographically realistic, while Crane's own was strongly interior, photographically (really cinematically before cinema) symbolic. Compare the concluding chapters of the two novels for key likenesses and differences.

The Characters
of *Maggie*

The characters of *Maggie* are basically the members of the Johnson family. Here is the Every Family of its kind of tenement neighborhood. That neighborhood is of course a teeming one, yet Crane almost isolates the microcosm from its totality; the neighbors serve only as chorus for comment and evidence that, however extreme the Johnsons may be, they are so only in degree, not kind.

The book begins with Jimmie, already struggling for survival in a boy's world where physical prowess is measured in beatings not in stickball scoring. He must battle his own blockmates as well as gangs from nearby blocks. And so he is prepared for survival in the familial and workaday world he enters upon the death of his father. From his earlier pummelings of Maggie he grows to a recognition of her as "different," partly because she "blossomed in a mud-puddle" and partly because he has some vague tribal notion that one's own sister is mysteriously set aside from those of others. The latter probably stemmed from the melodramas of the time and the equally melodramatic songs: "You wouldn't dare insult me, sir, if Jack were only here." The distinction can be said to include mothers, for he may see his own mother as a "drunken fool," yet he subdues her, when forced to, differently from the flattening he would award a male counterpart.

Actually, he fears his mother too, from his youthful seeking out the safety of the old woman's apartment to the submission to his mother's dicta regarding Maggie, his fluttering conscience notwithstanding. And despite his boasting that he knows no fear except the "respect" he holds for fire engines, he is afraid of those he knows to be stronger, like Pete, for whose demolition he enlists fighting Billie. Jimmie has his mother's aggressiveness, without her reduction of it into senseless alcohol-frenzy. He has his father's calm, without the weak compulsion to prove himself the drunken equal of the mother. He has learned the ropes of his tough environment; his bulldogged obtuseness will see his truck, team and self through to delivery, dependably though without dispatch.

The mother, ironically Mary, is the matriarch that rules father and son. Her power of hand, tongue and will are rarely blunted and never quite subdued. In alcoholic rages she becomes all superhuman strength within subhuman vessel. But she has a poetic and prophetic side: her invectives and lamentations are biblical in background; her curses and keening, poetry from an immemorial past. She lives her life so drugged that no sensibilities she does not herself allow ever get through to her. Hers is successful survival not through competition primarily, but through escape so insularly perfect, it makes her every word sincere.

Still, what prompts all the endless round of rum, tirade and thrashing into utter exhaustion? Do these not represent senseless defiance of an environment she has no wit or way to alter, a blind frenzy against an ever imminent despair?

In this double sense, she is given a truly great moment in literature. Her final apostrophe of forgiveness, one not hers to give, blends the irrational truth in life and the mock heroic in art in an ending perfectly appropriate to both.

The father evidently does well enough at whatever job he has to support the family in the meagre fashion of the neighborhood. He seems never to have known anything different, and so accepts his social and economic fate with "applewood serenity." Sometime he must have courted the mother; sometime she must have been a likelier choice. Was he then rather like Maggie and she rather like Jimmie?

Certainly there are no ifs about his inability to cope with Mary's persistent will. And whatever sense of gentleness seems possible to him has been largely displaced by the convenient neighborhood methods of control: curses, threats, kicks, beatings. When these controls fail, escape drinking and consequent brawls take over. The monotony of such life is broken only by the scarcely less monotonous occurrence of mere death. He died.

The book, through author and characters, insists so

strongly upon the difference of Maggie from the rest, that a look at the similarity might prove balancing.

Early in the novel she is taking care of Tommie. She drags him along pavement, steps and floor; she, too, knocks him down. She seems more concerned with Jimmie's wounds than with Tommie's wails. She takes on the coloring of environmental pugilistic protection, for Pete is first of all to her a physical master of his scene. When she is introduced to his glamor, the glamor of his world—a world that knows no cooking, sewing or childbearing—she accepts it at face value because she wants to, because it fits her dream-world. And finally, when she is rejected by both "home" and "hero," she never once entertains the notion of a return to the collar factory or any equivalent. The environment has its stranglehold upon her, faithlessness of Pete and pride of family aside. Too, the revised edition saves her from final solicitations which readers almost instinctively must have felt beyond her. Crane wanted to drive the point home still more mercilessly—the environment had claimed her utterly, as it claims all in one way or another.

Now to consider her more usual side: she *was* "different"—more sensitive, more inwardly beautiful, more affectionate, less adaptable, more at the mercy of what others grew callouses to cover. Because she can neither resign herself nor escape Rum Alley in the usual ways, she gives up; or rather, she is forced to give up. Her very difference (and it too is one of degree, not kind) determine her end from the beginning. Note the choices: Jimmie says she'll either go to work or you know where. She goes to work. Once she has seen a totally different world, more starved for such as her difference made her, she cannot go back to that world of work. When she cannot really do the other either, the river or some equivalent becomes inevitable. Perhaps one should not say some equivalent, for even the murky, unclean river must have seemed instinctively a cleansing solution after the scrofulous males she passes enroute.

The other characters are only the typical impingements on this Every Family: boys for the daughters; girls for the sons; friends for both; and the encountering of people who represent something better in life— Pete for Maggie, Nell for Pete, the man from Buffalo for Nell. Lower Bowery looks to upper Bowery, looks to 14th Street, looks to Fifth Avenue. The look in the other direction is almost always one of easy money, ready sex, slumming thrill.

The other characters are typical also in the extent to which they are revealed. The more casual our encounter with people, the less we know of them. Crane holds realistically to this experiential point of view. His characters know of those they meet only that to which they are exposed and that which they really want to know and believe.

All in all, the real protagonist is the slum environment. It exacts economic and social subservience to the point of submissiveness ("Withered persons, in curious postures of submission to something . . .",

Chapter 2), of channeled defiance (Jimmie on the truck), of adaptability to circumstances (most, though especially Nell), of escape via alcohol (Father) or dreams (Maggie), or of blind destructive violence (Mary). All the seeming assertions of will over the environment are, however, merely illusory. All those who think they are making a good thing of it are but fooling themselves. If the description of the tenement block in chapter 2 is echoed from Dreiser and Eliot to the contemporary jungle school as the typical urban wasteland, it is only because all here is death-in-life, death by attrition, until the actuality comes almost as mercy.

The Red Badge of Courage

Structural Outline

Chapters 1-2: Henry's recruit regiment awaiting its first action

Chapters 3-13: The first day's action and Henry's cowardice

Chapters 14-15: Re-assembled regiment in camp, awaiting the second round

Chapters 16-23: The second day's action and Henry's courage

Chapter 24: Withdrawal of the regiment from battle and Henry's afterthoughts

Chapter One:

A regiment is encamped, with the usual griping about inactivity. Chapter 2 has it on the move, but only for days of marching. Chapter 3 has it marching on the double and beginning to encounter skirmishing near the front. The story rests primarily with "the youth" Henry and is seen in great part through his senses and consciousness. However, the author-narrator stays just outside the protagonist.

1. What season of year does the novel open on? Do you think this is of any significance?

2. The second paragraph develops the acquisition of the tall soldier's story. What points to the possibility of the tale also being a tall one?

3. What rumor did the tall soldier pass on?

4. Look at the first four paragraphs again; list all the color words, as well as words which suggest color indirectly; then describe the overall scene in terms of colors only.

5. Why would there be a debate over whether the army was going to move or not?

6. What tense does the story begin with? Is this a usual tense for such a purpose? Why or why not?

7. "There was a youthful private who . . ." introduces a longer passage devoted to a single person. Do you think this points to his being an important character?

8. Where does the tense change and to what tense? What does the change indicate?

9. What notion had the young man had of the nature of war?

10. Why did he think he would not experience a war? Does the fact that a war came after all make his beliefs seem ironical?

11. Why had the young man wanted to enlist? Why had his mother discouraged him?

12. How had his mother taken the news of his enlistment? Does this show anything about her character?

13. Notice how casually the name of "the young man" is revealed. Why, do you suppose?

14. Do you think Henry's mother's advice had been typically motherly? Why or why not? Would you say that any of it had been sensibly practical?

Research Question:

In Shakespeare's *Hamlet* Polonius bids his son farewell as the latter is about to leave for the continent. Compare his farewell with Henry's mother's for common and varying points made.

15. Henry believed he enlisted of his own free will. Go back over what reasoning he used to ascertain whether you agree with him.

16. Would Henry have remembered his mother's whole speech word for word? Did you raise this question as you read it? An author cannot reproduce the actual utterly in his work. He has to select and create the illusion of reality.

Research Question:

Take any longer descriptive paragraph from Mark Twain's *Huck Finn*, a story Huck himself is telling. List expressions you think typical of him and those you think are not quite in character. Do you question these as you read ordinarily? How has Twain managed to create the illusion of reality?

17. Henry recalls how he had been treated as a hero all the way to army camp. Is there any contemporary parallel to this during an actual war?

18. What ideas of war had come back to him in the monotony of camp life?

19. What experiences had he had with the enemy? with his own frontline men?

20. When does the tense change again? What have we had between the past change of tense and this one? What is the name given to such a technique, especially in film and television plays?

21. What has Henry's look backward given the reader?

22. Before the reminiscence, "He had wished to be alone with some new thoughts that had lately come to him," what problem concerned him most?

23. This concern prompts another change of tense, another flashback. Is this a natural thing for us to do? Cite evidence for your answer.

24. Why do you suppose Henry's very tentmates are identified as "the tall soldier" and "the loud one," though their names are dropped in casually?

25. When Henry raised his own primary problem with Jim, why do you think the latter talked about the regiment as "they"? Do you think Jim's answer is realistic? Why or why not? How does it echo Henry's mother? Jim mentions Richmond and Johnnies. Have you known all along what war is taking place? If so, how did you know? Why, do you suppose, the author does not identify war, place and battle more precisely?

26. Why should the loud one be skeptical of all Jim Conklin says?

27. Why is Henry now reassured?

purled, sulkily, disdaining, oblique, secular, Homeric, impregnable, brindle, ordeal, vivacious, bland, Huns, broken-bladed glory, dexterously

Chapter Two

1. Jim Conklin's rumor turned out to be just that, and we have already noted how Crane prepared the reader for this possibility. Why would he do so in advance?

2. Jim Conklin had yesterday to defend his reliability orally and today, after the "sneering," he felt he had to beat up one of his critics. Is this at all normal, the degree to which he goes aside? Why or why not? Why should the author mention the critic as being from Chatfield Corners when we don't even know where Henry is from?

3. In *Maggie* we were close to the actual way of experiencing by several people, in fact almost in their consciousness: Jimmie, Pete, Nell, Mother and of course mainly Maggie. Here we are evidently going to see events primarily from whose consciousness?

4. Henry recognized that proof of his problem lay only where (note the comparison to the chemist)?

5. What term did he return to in his thinking of what present war really is? Define for yourself what the two words both denote and connote.

6. For what reasons did he tend to take Jim Conklin's word about standing one's ground *versus* running away?

7. If misery loves company, its kin uncertainty does too. Why did Henry not find somebody else as worried about his possible bravery under fire as Henry was about his?

8. Why should he classify his companions into only two extremes, heroes or doubters, especially after a possible middle ground had been pointed out by Jim Conklin?

9. What was his reaction to himself when he doubted those about him who were eager for battle?

10. Was he himself at all eager for battle? How do you know?

11. When you combine Henry's strain of thought (and there is a pun intended) and the title of the book, what do you come up with as probably the primary concern of the story?

12. One morning the regiment finally formed ranks and once more we have a description largely in color. How would you characterize the pattern of the colors as Henry sees them? Does it go with any of his previous thinking about war?

13. What are "the red eyes across the river" mentioned earlier and here twice? Why should eyes be used in the metaphor (figurative analogy)?

14. Why would Henry particularly wonder what a box of cigars had to do with war?

15. As the regiment swung into line, "it was now like one of those moving monsters wending with many feet." Instead of like what? What other animal term is used of it here?

16. Why should the men be so involved in guessing

at the strategy and be so full of merry speeches, while Henry concentrated on "his own eternal debate"? Was he so different from them?

17. The fat soldier's teasing wrangle with the young girl about the horse so engrossed all hands that "they entirely ceased to remember their own large war." How does this relate to the box of cigars?

18. If you were to think of fictional point of view as camera angle, where would it be in the camp scene that night? Why should this be a time for Henry to be homesick?

19. Why do you think the loud soldier, here first identified as Wilson, was so cocksure and mockmodest? Why did he and Henry resent each other's attitudes?

20. Meanwhile others were playing cards. Does Henry more and more appear to be the exception? Give reasons for your answer.

Research Question:

Greek literary accounts of wars were told in epic form, as in *The Iliad*. These began *in medias res*, in the middle of things, then went back for exposition, including roll calls of the leaders of both sides, Greeks and Trojans. The rosters continue in more modern adaptations, *Paradise Lost* (Forces of Christ and Satan) and *Moby Dick* (whalers and whales). Why, do you think, does Crane deliberately avoid such characteristics of epic form?

  scoffing, prolongation, fathom, unscrupulous, equipments, blatant, vociferous, "skedaddled"

Chapter Three

1. Once more a description largely in colors appears. What colors have been most frequently used? for describing what and how? From now on keep a simple color record, including words that suggest color or shading (lurid, darkness, gleam; and objects that have definite color, such as faces, gun barrels, uniforms—when they are deliberately used as part of the color impression).

2. One of the requirements of an army is camping; another, marching. Did the second sit any better with the men? What did it prompt them to do enroute?

3. How are veteran regiments distinguishable from new ones?

4. Henry returned to his notion of war as "a blue demonstration." In what respects is this not quite as true now as before?

5. A third requirement of an army is "marching on the double." How is the eternal gripe evidenced also in this by the men?

6. Henry's doubt began to turn into fear. What are the signs of the change?

7. What does Crane mean by "there were iron laws of tradition and law on four sides. He was in a moving box"?

8. "Across the river and into the trees" the regiment moved, finding skirmishings there. Why did Henry feel it was "a wrong place for a battlefield"?

9. How did the dead enemy soldier affect the men?

10. Henry wanted to stare at the dead man: "the

impulse of the living to try to read in dead eyes the answer to the Question." Is this Question the question bothering Henry regarding his courage? Give reasons for your answer.

11. Why is the private's feeling about generals' stupidity natural?

12. War is called "a red animal" and Henry terms the lieutenant who prodded him with his sword "a mere brute." How do these go with "the cathedral light of a forest"?

13. Why should there be a question about digging in? Must they not have had this as part of their training?

14. When the regiment's line was shifted three times during the morning, what do the men conclude? How would *you* account for such shifts?

15. Henry insisted upon the notion of "a blue demonstration." Where does the difference lie between change in his mind and change in actuality?

16. Why does Jim Conklin, "the tall man," seem more sensible than Wilson, "the loud soldier"? Does the use of the characterizing adjectives make any contribution to such an attitude on the part of the reader?

17. Does it make any sense that Henry should think hopefully of a quick death? Why or why not?

18. Is there anything to account psychologically for the change in attitude of "the loud soldier"? How do the expressions "girlish lip," "old boy," "quavering sob of pity," and "yellow envelope" contribute to creating an attitude in the reader?

19. How does Wilson's "glance as from the depths

of a tomb" parallel Henry's just-previous "He must look to the grave for comprehension"?

20. Chapter divisions are part of art rather than life, for in life particulars seem to be part of the general flow. Here one might expect to find Chapter Two containing all the marching and Chapter Three only the double march to the front. Why do you suppose Crane divides the chapters in the way he does?

perambulating, harangue

Chapter Four:

Chapters 4 and 5 describe the regiment's move up to the front, to find the one they are replacing in partial flight from a partial bending of one flank. The veteran regiments to either side and the recruits withstand the enemy charge. Henry also comes through well, by turns an automaton, an enraged brute, and the subject of a blurred daze.

1. Why would rumors run strongly among the men even during battle?

2. Of what significance is the mention here of Bill whose hand had been stepped on and of which doctors wanted to amputate three fingers?

3. The above mention is followed almost immediately by another hand wound (why the juxtaposition, do you think?), that of the lieutenant. How does this affect the recruits? why?

4. What happened as the flank of the regiment they are reinforcing was partly turned?

5. Note that some retreated "dissolved into a mob-like body of men who galloped like wild horses." We have noted animal metaphors applied to the men before. Keep a running list of such from now on.

6. As the officers vainly tried to stem the tide, why, do you think, did one mounted officer in his rage display "the anger of a spoiled child"?

7. Why is the partial retreat described as a "mad current" and the officers as "carried along on the stream like exasperated chips"?

8. With what "one desire" are "the eyes wild"?

9. Do you think Henry's thinking that he would run when he encountered "the composite monster" might be prophetic?

Chapter Five:

1. Why should Henry be thinking of his youthful waiting for the circus and "a thousand details of color and form" as he (the regiment) awaits attack?

2. Note here additions to your lists of color and animal analogies. We had better start a third list, of which we have already noted some instances: that of references to men acting like children (Henry going back to childhood memories is one kind: the captain talking to the men as a schoolmistress to children. Note also Henry's fight for air, and the man at his elbow, babbling.)

3. Once worried about his gun being loaded, Henry now loads like what?

4. Do you think Henry experiences the battle brotherhood deliberately or subconsciously? on what evidence?

5. Earlier Henry felt himself boxed in; now he "was like a carpenter . . . making still another box." What is implied?

6. What do the following sentences tell about Henry's experience? "And these jolted dreams were never perfect to him afterward, but remained a mass of blurred shapes. . . . The youth in his battle sleep heard this as one who dozes hears."

7. After identification with fellows "came a red rage", "mad feeling," "anger," "heated rage," "wild barbaric song," "babbled idiotically" all with assorted descriptive elements. What kind of behavior is indicated? Here is the fourth category for your list—images of madness, of the irrational.

8. Why is so much made of the unheroic postures of the men and the unpicturesque behavior of the officers?

9. Why did the blubbering coward not run anyhow after he could not hold his gun still long enough to load without help from the lieutenant?

10. Are the images of men being hit heroic? Why do you think so many who are hit fall with sad or unbelieving looks? How about the positions of the dead?

11. What had the regiment accomplished, even after they had witnessed the partial retreat of those they had come to support? Do you think it is im-

portant that in a sense the recruits had some veterans among them, not merely seasoned regiments on their flanks?

12. As the men rested, the big guns continued the fight. How are they described? What is the figure of speech used to do this called?

13. In the lull, Henry noticed two things: (1) the extent of the battle; and (2) the beauty of Nature roundabout. What do these add to Henry's concept of the fighting?

14. Earlier we noted a reference to "the cathedral light of a forest." Here Henry notes the beauty of nature "in the midst of so much devilment." From your present vantage point in the story do you think the author is suggesting that nature is good and man is evil?

15. The images of a battle are myriad, swift and jumbled. As Henry himself noted, most of them are not part of a conscious encounter. May this fact help explain why the author preferred to be ostensibly within Henry and yet to write in the third person? Discuss.

imprecations

Chapter Six:

This chapter marks a turning point as Henry, along with many others, runs when faced by the second wave of the attack. He thinks he has done the wise and general thing, for he who runs away today will be alive to fight another day. But in his flight he comes upon the division general celebrating the fact that the center (Henry's section) has held.

1. Is it easier to feel a bond in sharing victory than defeat? Does Henry's present feeling "the bonds of tied hearts" differ from "the subtle battle brotherhood" during the attack?

2. Should the men have been surprised at a renewal of the attack? Do you suppose their basic training pointed up such a possibility?

3. What echo do you find in "I didn't come here to fight the hull damn' rebel army?"

4. Why did Henry notice particularly the enemy flag advancing "resplendent"?

5. To the earlier image of Henry and the others "fighting like automations" must now be added the fact that the enemy "must be machines of steel," "machine-like fools." Here is a fifth category to watch cumulatively, men imaged as machines.

6. Was Henry braver than the others, since some had already dropped their guns and run when he did so?

7. Did Henry run of his own free will? Explain.

8. As he retreated "with the zeal of an insane sprinter," he entered the zone of the enemy's shelling. The shells seemed to scream, to be grinning at him with cruel teeth, while his own batteries were "disputing" and their guns "spoke with dogged valor." (Note others along here). We noticed this strain of images earlier and now add them to our list as cat-

egory No. 6—machines personified, imaged in human terms. How does this relate to category 5—men imaged as machines?

9. What did Henry learn from the general that related directly to him?

10. Which of our categories does the concluding maneuver of the general belong to?

formidable, cantering, blanched, livid, groveled

Chapter Seven:

Chapters 7—11 mark Henry's retreat, physical in part, mental in far greater part, as he seeks to justify his cowardice while others stayed to hold the day. He finds comfort in nature, only to be suddenly brought face to face with an open-eyed seated corpse being explored by ants. Then chameleon-like he seeks to join the column of the wounded, only to see Jim Conklin die and "the tattered man" go wound-crazy. Again he runs and wrestles with himself.

1. Up to this point Henry had felt retreat not only reasonable but the only alternative to sheer collective suicide. What now enters his mental state?

2. How could Henry feel "that he had been wronged"? What mental process do you see setting in here? This is the first of a series of "outs" from his mental predicament.

3. The very forest in which he sought refuge sought to turn to hold him back. What psychological process is at work here? Here is Henry's second out.

4. Retarding obstructive nature turns almost too readily to favorably inclined, peaceful Nature. Here is a counterpoint central to the whole technique of the novel. When Henry projects his inner disturbances—dreams, guilt, rages of war—we get an expressionistic canvas of associational montage, distortion, fragmentation, exaggeration, and even utter turnabout. When Henry senses the unity about him—in nature, in the broad disposition of the battlefield, in the unitedly victorious sector—we get the impressionistic canvas of patterned color and light. Crane's impressionism has been documented from the very first; his equally prevalent expressionism has seldom, and developmentally never, been remarked.

Research Question:

Look up the characteristic sociological representations of the dramatic expressionism of Strindberg, the Germans of the 1920's, O'Casey, O'Neill and ascertain which ones are found here in Crane.

5. What help did he get from throwing a pine cone at a squirrel? from the small animal pouncing into the swamp water and emerging with a fish? Henry's third out is explicit here.

6. Why did he seek out the thickest thickets?

7. At one point in his retreat he reaches a natural bough-formed chapel, as earlier he had encountered "the cathedral light of a forest." Where do his cathedral-chapel notions stem from? Any evidence of his having any religious background? Does his behavior suggest any kind of ethical upbringing?

8. Ironically, what did he discover in the "chapel"?

Still more ironical, where was "the thing," that is, what would be where "it" was in an actual chapel? Earlier we raised the question whether Crane meant to suggest that nature is good and man is evil; how does this incident bear on the question? What fourth out did this contrast give Henry?

9. Why, psychologically, should he have "received a subtle suggestion to touch the corpse"?

sagacious, conciliate

Chapter Eight:

1. Once more the "devotional" quiet of nature is disturbed by the roar of war.

Research Question:

Compare the natural settings of chapters 7 (end) and 8 (beginning) with that of Wordsworth's sonnet, "It Is A Beauteous Evening, Calm and Free." Is the outlook on nature the same? Can we separate Henry's from Crane's notion of nature?

2. Henry sees irony in his situation, discovering the necessity of illusion for men in war. How can this be adjudged his fifth out?

3. Now the seeming shackles of nature are interpreted as another (the sixth) out. What is it?

4. Is his urge to go toward the voice of battle the proverbial psychological one of being drawn to the scene of his crime?

5. Why did Henry hurry by the little field of dead but join the lengthening column of the wounded?

6. What did "the tattered man" wish from Henry?

For a different reason, was Henry not in the same position? Explain.

7. What does the tattered man's dialect tell about him? Have you found any dialect similar to that in *Maggie?* Why or why not, do you suppose?

8. Why do you suppose Henry could not lie when the tattered man asked him whether he had been hit? transfixed, medley, perfunctory, stupendous

Chapter Nine:

1. Why do you suppose Crane has not referred before to the obvious title and does so first just here?

2. Interpret the phrase "dragging their own tragedies toward the rear," thinking of "tragedies" in both its actual and artistic senses.

3. Why was Henry seemingly so glad to see Jim Conklin?

4. Why did Jim literally cling to Henry out of fear? Since Jim had stood his ground well throughout the battle, what is the reader meant to pick up here about fear?

5. How rational is Jim during this episode? Discuss.

6. As "the tattered man" and Henry watched Jim "They began to have thoughts of a solemn ceremony. There was something ritelike in these movements of the doomed soldier. And there was a resemblance in him to a devotee of a mad-religion, blood-sucking, muscle-wrenching, bone-crushing." Are his actual death throes "ritelike"? How can they be physiologically and psychologically accounted for?

7. Of what that resembles a mad religion is Jim really a fanatic victim, remembering previous uses of the adjectives? What actually has transformed him into a fanatic here?

8. At what is Henry shaking his fist? Is that also against what he seems about to deliver a philippic?

9. The philippic reduced itself to "Hell—." It is followed only by the image of the red sun "pasted in the sky like a wafer." Does the latter go with the other religious uses of nature ("cathedral light of a forest," wood chapel)? What particular religious rite may the final image be an allusion to? If so, how does it relate to Henry's "Hell—" and fist shaking?

10. Essentially the men fighting here are in what religious tradition, many doubtless actual adherents? Does this fact suggest that the sun image and/or the other similar nature images may be ironical? Discuss.

Research Question:

Because his death is focal and his initials are JC, Jim Conklin has sometimes been interpreted as a Christ figure in the novel. Compare the story of Christ and that of Conklin for literal and figurative similarities and differences, remembering that the latter must have some base in the former. Decide whether Jim is a parallel sacrificial figure for Jesus, not overlooking the possibility of an ironic parallel, not forgetting the chapter's concluding image, and finally not forgetting the essential of uniqueness.

helitywhoop, ague, philippic

Chapter Ten:

1. How do you suppose "the tattered man" could talk about pea soup after what he has just witnessed? Might this go with the box of cigars, with the incident of the men forgetting about the war in the fat man's teasing attempt to steal the horse, in the card playing on the eve of battle, and in the general's "carnival of joy" after the center held? Discuss.

2. Jim Conklin's end had shown Henry another side of fear—that it could come after, as well as before and during. Now what did "the tattered man" teach him about fear with his story about Tom Jamison and himself?

3. Give as many reasons as you can why "the tattered man" is particularly tough for Henry's conscience.

4. What did he wish as an out now that pseudo-identification with the wounded had not helped? Since he had once thought of this out earlier, before the regiment had come through the first wave of the attack, has he come full circle now?

5. Our questions have related to the different versions of fear manifested by Henry's comrades and himself. Can we tally any equivalent series of kinds of courage shown? The fear is hardly a matter of free will; is the courage? Give reasons for your answer.

Chapter Eleven:

1. How can Henry know of the battle roadway scene that "Fear was sweeping it all along"? Does this thought give him another out in his rationalizing process?

2. How is the two-way traffic of wagons reminiscent of *Maggie?*

3. The fresh column forging to the front brought Henry to near despair. He had seen such before; why should this time be so much harder? Is there a clue in his newest attribution of blame?

4. An earlier out in Henry's catalogue of rationalization was the wish to be dead; what wish fulfillment images now dominate him?

5. Almost these wishes succeed; what objections stand in the way of his urge to rejoin his group? What does further rationalization do to him?

6. What do you suppose is meant by "A certain mothlike quality within him kept him in the vicinity of the battle? Does this have any bearing on our repeated question regarding freedom of the will in Henry's actions?

7. When he gave up on himself, did hope die utterly or did he find something else to pin it on?

8. What phrase here deliberately sums up the fear side, the opposite of "the red badge of courage"?

9. He rejects his latest out with revulsion, even thinking himself the "murderer" of many soldiers. Such nearness to despair can bring on only what

wish again? What is this wish the contrary of? Do the two psychologically go together?

10. What is implicit in his referring now to "the mighty blue machine" instead of "the blue demonstration"?

11. Why do you suppose it is so difficult for him to lie? Does the difficulty lie within him, outside of him, or both? Discuss.

12. Why is his imagined scene at the end of the chapter a typical expressionistic rather than an impressionistic one? Would you say that the chapters of his retreat have been more strongly expressionistic or impressionistic? Explain.

Research Question:

Hawthorne's *The Scarlet Letter* begins structurally with the exterior and goes deeper and deeper into those concerned reaching its interior climax in the Chapter XI, "The Interior of a Heart." Is there a structural parallel in the deepening of inner exploration here in Henry? Does Henry too, like Dimmesdale, finally have to take his place where his conscience leads him? Are there salient differences?

Chapter Twelve:

This chapter marks a turning point, for Henry receives a wound, though not at all as a mark of courage. Under the debilitating effects of it and his "longest day," he is helped back to his old regiment by an unknown soldier.

1. Literally inundated by a new retreat, Henry "forgot that he was engaged in combating the universe. He threw aside his mental pamphlets on the philosophy of the retreated and rules for the guidance of the damned." What does Crane suggest by both meaning and tone here?

2. When "the man" whom Henry clung to for explanation hit him over the head with the butt of his rifle, Henry's fingers "turned to paste upon the other's arm." On his death march Jim Conklin's face (he was earlier called "the spectral soldier") "turned to a semblance of gray paste" and later "The red sun was pasted in the sky like a wafer." Are these uses of paste merely repetitive or do they form a purposeful, if subconscious, pattern?

3. Was Henry's wound really so serious as to cause him so much difficulty? And how and why did he go "tall soldier fashion"?

4. Why would scenes of home and early summer pursuits pop into Henry's head now? And why would he be so tired?

5. The man who took Henry in hand is given a whole monologue, including answers to what Henry evidently says to him. Why does Crane give us only the man's part? How does this relate to the essential point of view of staying as close to Henry's consciousness as possible?

6. Why did the last words of his friend Jack strike "the man" as odd? What is the function of telling the incident at this point?

7. Is it significant that the one who took Henry back to his regiment remained utterly unknown to Henry?

altercations, gesticulating, ruck

Chapter Thirteen:

Chapters 13-15 find Henry back at his own campfire, a very full 24 hours later. Once having lied about his wound, he becomes glib at lying, criticism and self-pride, so that because of what he knows about Wilson and what Wilson does not know about him, the relationship between the two undergoes a psychological reversal.

1. How is Henry able to lie now, when he could let his "wound" speak for itself, even though he could not lie earlier, before "the man with the cheery voice" steered him to the regimental camp? How do you account for him actually becoming glib at telling the lie of being shot?

2. Is it significant that Simpson believes the lie yet diagnoses the wound correctly?

3. The campfire scene represents a perfect blend of impressionistic and expressionistic description. Which is which, and how are they interwoven?

4. What do you think has changed Wilson from "the loud soldier" to the solicitous one here? Why is he now referred to as "the friend"?

5. We have returned to the scene at the beginning of Chapter Three, one evening later. You might well recapitulate what has intervened, quite a day.

Chapter Fourteen:

1. Why do you think Henry is made to undergo the momentary illusion of being among the dead? Need we invoke his frequent deathwish of yesterday to properly appreciate his present scare?

2. After coming to, Henry "swore a complicated oath at himself." This is the first mention of any such since his mother's warning about the perils of the army. Why do you think Crane uses the word "complicated" and the preposition "at"?

3. Interestingly, here we have the first sustained dialogue of Henry since Chapter Two. As his vernacular reappears, do you have trouble putting the speaker together with all his inner chatter of the intervening chapters? Do they jibe entirely? Perhaps it would be easier to think of the two as one and the same person if we remind ourselves about the levels of consciousness at which he has been functioning at various times. Discuss.

4. Do you think the salutary change Henry noted in Wilson may subconsciously affect him too? Explain.

5. Why did Wilson refer to "those days," speaking "as after a lapse of years"?

6. Henry's "Why, lord, man, you didn't see nothing of the fight" is interrupted by his revealing Jim Conklin's death. Is the "sudden thought" only this, or is he remembering his own yesterday, or remembering the changes in Wilson, or what?

7. Why does Wilson hate to see "th' boys fightin' 'mong themselves"?

8. How does Wilson's last speech leave the door open nicely for Henry?

petulantly, deprecatory

Chapter Fifteen:

1. How does Crane's new term "the friend" become even more meaningful in terms of Henry's thought about the yellow envelope?

2. Does the resurgence of Henry's self-pride so quickly and strongly seem plausible?

3. Henry could of course not rationalize away his fleeing. How did he make it palatable?

4. Why should there seem to be a seemingly complete psychological reversal in Henry and Wilson respectively?

lugubrious, ejaculates

Chapter Sixteen:

Chapters 16-23 mark the second day of Henry Fleming's regiment under fire. The round of events is similar to yesterday's, though the men begin the action with less vigor but more experience. Successively they move up to the skirmish area; charge in battle frenzy; are said to fight like mule drivers and therefore declared expendable for a tough sector; advance over forest and beyond the line of veterans who kid them accordingly; withdraw over the terrain just won; and withstand two counter attacks to retake a protective rail fence fallen to the enemy.

Through it all Henry and Wilson fight in various states of frenzy, following each of which they gain a bit more in perspective.

1. When the regiment was pulled up to the trenches, Henry wanted to joke while the rest were full of only doleful and direful rumors. Why this difference?

2. The withdrawal of the group gave rise to another round of gripes regarding the generalship. Who should know better and why? What is the double irony here?

3. What echoes in the remark by the "sarcastic man" shook Henry?

4. Henry "became suddenly a modest person." We have seen him by turns as dreamer, grumbler, doubter, firebrand, coward, rationalizer, cock of the walk, and now "modest person." Did he wilfully choose and become any of these or was he made into them by background, environment and circumstances? Discuss.

5. Why do you suppose Henry cannot seem to stay "modest" for long?

6. How do you interpret the conclusion: "They stood as men tied to stakes"?

fracas, temerity

Chapter Seventeen:

1. What mood was Henry in for this day's scrap?

2. How does yesterday's initial assault repeat itself in Henry's firing?

3. How did Henry become suddenly "a war devil"? How would you characterize his present courage?

4. Interpret: ". . . he was now what he called a hero. And he had not been aware of the process. He had slept, and, awakening, found himself a knight."

5. Did Henry do anything for the troops with his zealousness?

6. Why would the sky now be described artificially as "blue enamelled"?

exasperation, spasmodic

Chapter Eighteen:

1. What is the significance of Rogers' getting shot before the fight he has challenged Wilson to can come off?

2. Is going after water for Rogers and the others a plausible reason for having Henry come across his second general in two days?

3. What is meant by the officer's remark that the 304th fight like mule-drivers?

4. Why do Wilson and Fleming not tell the men all that they overheard, but only that they were going to charge?

Chapter Nineteen:

1. As Henry swung into the charge "he looked to be an insane soldier." How does this description relate to his prior conduct under fire?

2. Explain Henry's illusion "that he saw everything" in utter clarity?

3. Crane describes the charge as "the delirium that encounters despair and death, and is heedless and blind to the odds. It is a temporary but sublime absence of selfishness." What does the second sentence add here to what has repeatedly been stated in terms of children, beasts, and madness? Do you think the line may be one of those that prove prophetic?

4. How did the assault, once halted by lack of breath and momentum, get going again? How is the tree-to-tree warfare typically American?

5. Did Henry and Wilson deliberately lead the charge across the last strip of open ground? Explain.

6. Does Henry's feeling about the flag here relate to the second sentence of the quotation in question 3?

    accoutrements

Chapter Twenty:

1. Why could nothing get the regiment moving forward again after falling back to the shelter of the trees?

2. What had kept Henry helping the lieutenant try to get the regiment moving once more?

3. Why is the regiment called "a machine run down"?

4. Why should a counterattack not have been a surprise to the regiment?

5. What is the significance of the last sentence, "And they were men"? Is this the feeling of Henry and the others, of Crane, or both?

Research Question:

Compared to post World War I and II fiction, Crane uses relatively little profanity. This limited use of it had also been characteristic of *Maggie*, and in the 1896 revision of that novel he cut out quite a bit. Do you think he was concerned about late Victorian readership?

Chapter Twenty-One:

1. Show that the regiment had really in a sense still been beside itself in the action just concluded.

2. Between the mule-drivers accusation of the higher officer and the sallies of the veterans as the regiment slunk back to their own lines where they really belonged, what added barbs came their way and from whom?

3. Do you think the colonel really said those things about Wilson and Fleming? If so, why did the lieutenant not report it?

swashbuckler

Chapter Twenty-Two:

1. What did Henry gain from the brief respite from activity when he had the chance to observe other portions of the battle line?

2. What ground was changing hands during these pitched battles that were but parts of the larger battlefield?

3. What is the primary objective, as illustrated by your answer to Question 2, of a battle?

4. Henry resolved that his dead body should lie as a reproach to the regiment's detractors. How does this square with "the most startling thing" he learned while eavesdropping on the general?

expletives, frowzled

Chapter Twenty-Three:

1. Why was the exhausted regiment ready to charge again, so soon after no plea whatever would register?

2. When Crane reiterates "again grown wild with an enthusiasm of unselfishness," are we to think that this is the feeling of the regiment only, and that the higher officers still think of them as "mule drivers" and "mud diggers"? Discuss.

Research Question:

There is a Washington sculpture, a replica of a photograph from World War II, Raising The Flag at Iwo Jima. Look up the background of the battle, especially the flag raising itself and compare it with the one in this chapter. Are flags still as coveted as then? Why or why not?

3. Why are the four prisoners brought into the story, in your judgment? Do they appear to be categorically representative? Do they parallel any types among the blues?

paroxysm, obdurate

Chapter Twenty-Four:

The regiment is withdrawn from the lines and front. Henry's new assurance is offset by guilt over his abandonment of the "tattered man." At the end, Henry feels they have become men and an outfit, a fact, and that from now on all is going to be all right, a youthful dream that further exposure to the job of day-after-day campaigning is sure to temper.

1. What ironic occurrence now comes as anti-climax?

2. Once again Henry's "brain emerged from the clogged clouds." Did he strike any balance beyond his earlier series of variations? How did he arrive at his present estimate?

3. What is supposed to be signified by Henry's "outburst of crimson oaths"?

4. Why should his desertion of "the tattered man" trouble Henry so, and his running from the battle and lying not at all? Why should he refer to it as a "sin"?

4. What is meant by "the brass and bombast of his earlier gospels," not overlooking a careful defining of "earlier."

5. The peroration of his thoughts with their release "to images of tranquil skies, fresh meadows, cool brooks—an existence of soft and eternal peace" [all there except mother's old fashioned apple pie]—aside, how do we separate what he has really acquired from what he thinks he has achieved? And shall we designate the learning process as conditioning? Is any of it the result of his free decision?

6. This chapter has sometimes been considered a novelistic anticlimax by critics. Do you think Crane intended it so? Do you feel it is necessary to the novel's aesthetic completeness? Is the military anticlimax pertinent here? Discuss.

Research Questions:

Does war then make men? Are men made only by war? What is the essential attitude toward war reflected by the unifying image patterns and by Henry's particular experience? Some of the research questions that follow should help you answer these questions satisfactorily if not definitively.

You have been recording images of soldiers acting like beasts, like children, like madmen (irrationally), and like machines. What is the one thing, therefore, that men in war do not act like? And yet they eventually emerge as what? How do you resolve this seeming contradiction?

Stanley B. Greenfield has called attention to another series of images unifying the novel, those of food and drink "stressing the survival theme" of "war as an eat-or-be-eaten affair." Even a casual count quickly reaches three dozen such images. Collect and interpret such images fully.

Throughout we have noted, without asking you to record, images of ordinary home life appearing at intervals. What are their psychological and aesthetic function in the novel, and are the two functions in concord?

Still another series of images are those belonging to the world of magic and the occult. Notable examples are omens, phantoms, specters, demons, imps, witch, magician, devils, genie, ghouls, and the vampire suggestion of blood-sucking. Establish the function of this image category.

Short fiction has to begin as near as possible to the central situation. Yet what goes before must give the necessary exposition or explanation for understanding that situation and the motivation of the participant in it. How does Crane achieve this, comparatively, in *Red Badge of Courage* and *Maggie?*

In *Maggie* we noted frequent use of synesthesia, especially in color images. Check the color imagery in this novel and compare its use, generally, in type and frequency with that in *Maggie*.

In *Maggie* we noted strains of imagery that were also used in *The Red Badge of Courage:* animal images, images of madness or irrationality, grown-ups acting like children. What are the comparative frustrations that account for such behavior? Would these evidence a naturalistic outlook in Crane?

From Crane's 1895 trip to Mexico came a small group of stories. Two of these are quite in the cowardice-courage vein of *The Red Badge of Courage*. Show comparatively how the New York Kid in "Five White Mice" and Richardson in "Horses—One Dash" attribute strength to others and fear to themselves, only to discover that fear depends on circumstances.

Research Question:

Study "Killing His Bear" in *The Sullivan Sketches*. Compare the technical point of view and its relation to the protagonist with that in *The Red Badge of Courage*.

Characterization in
The Red Badge of Courage

There is pre-eminently but one character, Henry Fleming. The entire novel literally *is* his cumulative development of a certain degree of courage, through a series of conditioning factors. One cannot characterize him without summarizing that development and therefore the book. Since, then, the stress here is almost exclusively on process, let us look at that process.

Henry begins in doubt about his ability to come through without cowardice. In a fighting frenzy he helps contain the first enemy charge, then caught with his psychological guard down, runs from the second one. He retreats with the comfortable rationalization that he has done the sensible, realistic thing against insuperable odds, only to find that his comrades had held. The realization prompts a whole series of psychological "outs" from his guilt, one after another to be found wanting, so that the death wish becomes almost a refrain-like recurrence.

Sheer circumstances get him hit over the head with the rifle butt of one from his own side. Here is the perfect rationalization for a return to his group, achieved at the end of the day through the offices of a "man with a cherry voice" whose face he never once sees.

Accepted in his regiment as a proven soldier, he feels compelled to prove himself to himself and others in fact during the next day's action. Keyed to battle frenzy, yet with a calm born of the previous day's partial conditioning, he comes through as a man in an outfit, not merely a soldier in the ranks. The transformation is cumulative; with each new wave of own or enemy assault he grows in battle awareness, essentially through subconscious feedback. He does not quite reach veteran stage, perhaps an obvious impossibility in two scant days, lacking at the end the cool resignation of those who fight because it is their job whenever and however called upon to do so.

Henry's domination of the book leads to the often asked question whether he is typical, a sort of Every Man undergoing his baptism of fire. Clearly what gives rise to the query is the elaborate mental process through which he goes. The point of view here, characteristically within yet without his consciousness, details the kaleidescopic stream of sensory images, central and peripheral, that comprise anyone's experience of battle. These and the equally detailed rationalizations necessary to justify his conduct in terms of conventional notions of cowardice and courage are experienced largely in the subconscious. Crane expresses a literary symbolical style deliberately in contrast to the youth's vernacular. Henry could not have the experiences themselves in these stylistic terms, but they seem truer to the images of the experiences than would the language in which he himself would describe them. Too, no single soldier is subjected to all the facets of battlefield experience, especially in two days, yet all the facets themselves are within the realm of probability for very soldier; and every day's action is a microcosm of the entire war.

In the sense that Henry is Every Man, or at least Every Enlisted Man, "the regiment" is Every Regiment in Any Battle of Every War. There is just enough localization to verify that every universal experience is necessarily shaped in the particularity of its own place and time.

But three men are central in Henry's battle odyssey. Two are his tentmates: Jim Conklin, whom he sees die a death of fear-and-fanaticism-filled courage; and Wilson, whom he sees change from loudmouthed braggart to quiet friend largely because somebody calls his bluff. The third, "the tattered man," haunts his conscience because he abandoned him to delirious wanderings brought on by wounds.

All the others appear only fragmentarily, as they impinge upon Henry's immediate moments: as fellow cheerleader for team effort, the lieutenant; as evidence that the battle was not merely an aimless mess, the general; as maddening insult that leads to frenzied courage, the captain who calls them expendable mule drivers; and even as disembodied bits of dialogue, the general chorus. Any intimacy is one of situation and its demands. You meet the faces that you meet as circumstances bring you together, friend or foe.

Poems and Short Stories

The Black Riders

VI—"God fashioned the ship of the world carefully."

1. How does "All-Master" square with what follows?

2. Relate the "for ever rudderless" to the naturalistic outlook already noted in Crane.

3. Is the attitude toward the universe here the same as that toward nature in *The Red Badge of Courage?* Compare the attitude here and that expressed in XXIX.

XLVI—"Many red devils ran from my heart"

1. What do you think "the red devils" are?

2. How does the image of redness here relate to its use elsewhere in Crane? Are all uses diabolical?

LI—"A man went before a strange God—"

1. Is this a contrast between an institutional and a personal God, between a supernatural notion of God and the human himself, or between God of Wrath and

God of Mercy? Discuss.

2. How does the concept of God here relate to that in VI above?

LIV—" 'It was wrong to do this,' said the angel."

1. Do you think all these poems about God and angels mean Crane really believed in them? How, then, can he be termed a naturalist? If on the other hand he does not believe in them, why is he using them?

2. How must man live in terms of "malice" and "war"? Explain. Compare the basic attitude here with that in XXIV and LXVI.

"The Veteran"

This story, published in *The Little Regiment* together with a group of war stories, presents Henry Fleming as a grandfather. The story also represents a meeting of the Whilomville kind of background, though a smaller and more rustic version, and the war characters.

1. Is there any significance to the similarity of the light in the grocery to that described in the tent at the beginning of *The Red Badge of Courage*?

2. Why is Henry here called "Mr. Fleming"?

3. Is Fleming's admission of cowardice an illustration of admitting what one can afford to admit? Discuss.

4. What had evidently happened to Henry sometime after his first battle and of what contribution is that to the present circumstances and to question 3?

5. Is his recall of himself as thinking himself the center of everything then accurate? Why should one ask the question?

6. Again, is his recall of Jim Conklin going "into it from the start just as if he was born to it" true?

7. Would Sickles's colt ordinarily interest little Jim? How do you know? What does the repetition of the question and its answer imply?

8. Was the Swede blubbery about the fire because he was drunk?

9. Why should Fleming's face become a gray mask of horror?

10. Who is "the old lady," do you suppose?

11. There was really no chance of saving the barn. What then were the hired men up to with their important bucket brigade from the reluctant well?

12. What had evidently happened to Fleming in freeing the horses? Would you call this an irony of fate? Discuss.

13. What is a "tocsin note"? What kind of figure of speech is it?

14. Crane writes "and then came this Swede again, crying as one who is the weapon of the sinister fates." How has this fact become apparent? Would it have been more effective to leave this implicit instead of making it explicit?

15. Is Fleming really heroic in going after the colts, or merely "absent-mindedly" old and sentimental?

16. Does this Fleming stem logically from the one of the novel? Discuss.

"The Open Boat"

As the subtitle indicates this story is a fictional re-telling of a factual occurrence. The steamer *Commodore*, filibustering arms from Jacksonville to Cuba, sprang a leak and began to fill. The men took to the boats, with the Captain, the cook, the oiler and Crane in the last one. The story relates the dinghy's struggle to reach shore, a part but briefly treated in the news account of the event filed by correspondent Crane.

I.

1. What is the camera angle, so to speak, of the narrator? How can you tell?
2. Why was the Captain dejected?
3. What equipment for maneuvering was aboard?
4. Is the agreement between cook and correspondent characteristic under the circumstances? Explain.
5. Whose is the realistic voice aboard?
6. Was there any other work to do besides steering?

II.

1. What is favorable and unfavorable about the weather? What other conditions could be supposed?
2. What is meant by "the ethics of their condition"? Does this relate to the previous question? How

is the phrase expressive of Crane's typical outlook?

3. Are gulls "ugly brutes"? Could the "ominous" gull be likened to the Ancient Mariner's albatross? Why or why not?

4. What was the courage-cowardice status of the four?

5. Who rowed? Why, do you suppose?

III.

1. How does "the subtle brotherhood of men that was here established on the seas" compare to the brotherhood of battle we have heard about? Does your answer suggest anything regarding whether war is necessary to make men?

2. Why does Crane go further in this story than heretofore in expressing his admiration of fellowmen?

3. Why are the topics of rest and food brought up?

4. How can they sit and smoke cigars after the oiler's remarks about the other boats?

IV.

1. What does the passage on Fate imply? Does it go with anything we have encountered before in Crane's work? What kind of pattern in outlook are we cumulatively finding expressed in this chronological survey of selected Crane works? Discuss.

2. What skillful maneuver did the oiler now have

to perform? Why is this so difficult, practically speaking?

3. How does Crane keep his point of view all through approximately the next two pages of dialogue?

4. There is a repetition of part of the earlier Fate passage. Who, do you think, is formulating this? Why is it stylistically such a far cry from the dialogue and even from the narrative prose? Can you apply any previous findings of our reading here?

V.

1. Why do you think Crane writes "These two lights were the furniture of the world"? Does this relate to the cook's remarks about pie and ham sandwiches?

2. How much depended upon a single man in this night of waiting it out?

3. Just when the correspondent thought he was the only being awake what company did he get? Why does he never identify "it"?

VI.

1. The narrator's outlook on nature continues to include the whole universe. Why do you think he uses the term "temple"?

2. Of what significance is it that art, even the rather mediocre verse he adduces here, is made mean-

ingful by life? What is happening in the telling of the story? What relationship between life and art is suggested?

3. Does the captain play any important role, lying there in the bow at rest?

VII.

1. The correspondent calls nature indifferent now. Is this really what he has implied thus far? If so, there's no change from the attitude in *The Red Badge of Courage*. Is there any resentment, if of the moment, to parallel the near-approach to such in some of the poems?

2. How are we to take the statement that "if he were given another opportunity he would mend his conduct, and be better and brighter during an introduction or at a tea"? In what words does the give-away lie?

3. "It merely occurred to him that if he should drown it would be a shame." What has brought on such a comedown from the previous cosmic concern?

4. Do you think the correspondent's feeling that drowning would after all be easy is plausible? Would the shoreline look so detail-clear to him? Why or why not?

5. Who can be interpreters of an experience? Only those? How does this relate to *The Red Badge of Courage?*

6. Was all the commentary on Fate primarily per-

sonal for the narrator? Why or why not? What about its application now to Billie, the oiler? Retrace the full irony of his death through the story. Since this death was a fact, do you think it influenced the narrator's attitude toward nature/universe? Discuss.

Research Question

Compare the story and the news account by Crane. Also, look up other newspaper accounts of the event to fill in details on the remainder of the crew. Why do you think Crane omitted the single act of cowardice, the first mate's irrationality, and concentrated entirely on the quiet courage of the four in the boat, especially since we have noted his tremendous interest in cowardice *versus* courage?

topmast, Canton-flannel gulls, painter, Sèvres, ninny-woman, obstreperous, cutwater

War Is Kind And Other Lines

III—"To the maiden"

1. How would you characterize the maiden's attitude toward the sea? the wrecked sailor's?

2. Is the "grim hatred of nature" only the sailor's or are we once more on a narrator's verge beyond "indifference"?

3. Compare this sea lyric with a development of the same general theme in I. of "Three Poems." What elements are left out and added in the latter?

XIV—"A slant of sun on dull brown walls,"

1. Does this poem suggest that all the universe, both nature and man, is purposeless and "senseless"? Do we have here an increase of bitterness (we termed it resentment earlier)? Compare XXI.

XXVI—"The trees in the garden rained flowers."

1. What does this fable in verse substitute for the Garden of Eden?

2. Does this poem relate directly to the survival of the fittest? If so, what fittest? If not, what is the analogy?

3. Who are represented respectively by "the father" and "the tutor"?

The Monster

Doctor Trescott's Negro stable boy rescues the Doctor's son Jimmie from his burning house, and his face is horribly disfigured by acid as he uses the laboratory as escape route. The Doctor insists on helping and caring for "The Monster," though most of Whilomville is eventually against him; he loses most of his practice and the women refuse to mix with his wife socially.

I.

1. What virtue does Jimmie manifest here?
2. Why does his father not reward him for his honesty?

II.

1. Where and how does Jimmie get solace on such occasions of parental "eclipse"?
2. How would you characterize the relationship between Henry and Jimmie?

III.

1. Of what import is it that Henry Johnson has a whole "dude" life aside from his work life, one that he himself treats utterly differently?
2. Are there any elements constant in the two Henry Johnsons? Discuss.
3. Why does the author say of the Farraguts and Henry that "if they had been occupants of the most gorgeous salon in the world they could not have been more like three monkeys."

IV.

1. Do you think Crane is building a kind of nostalgic picture of small town life deliberately? Know-

ing Crane rather well by now, what do you think this might all turn to, tonally?

2. What would the siren at this time indicate? Why does Crane not say so?

V.

1. Why do you suppose the hose carts were pulled by men instead of by teams as in *Maggie?*

2. Is all such curiosity about a fire natural in such a setting? How do you know?

3. This is one of Crane's stories about Whilomville, his fictitious name for the kind of small towns he spent his youth in—Port Jervis, New York; Paterson, New Jersey. What is he seeking to build in each story, therefore, aside from the strict development it requires? Would you think he wishes us to experience such small town life straight and/or ironically?

VI.

1. Why do you suppose Crane sketched in the Saturday night downtown scene and then turned to the Trescott fire, for obviously the latter came before the whistle that interrupted the band concert?

2. How could Mrs. Trescott not sense the fire when Hannigan choked on the smoke clear across the street? Are we catching Crane napping in creating the illusion of reality?

3. Where is the point of view in the story, primarily with any single individual? Discuss.

VII.

1. Why aren't we acquainted with what Henry is thinking and feeling, as is the usual case with Crane's protagonists? Why, above all, is there nothing at all said about cowardice and courage, though obviously we are once more involved in a test thereof?

2. What does Henry's sudden shift to helplessness mean? Why should his slavery roots be said to dictate his submission to the flames here?

3. Why should terror grip Henry precisely when he remembered the alternative escape route?

4. Is the laboratory fire scene expressionistic in intent and technique? Discuss.

VIII.

1. The general town activity precedes the switch to Dr. Trescott returning from a call. Why?

2. Why is the town not named until now?

3. Why did people restrain the Doctor from re-entering the house to go after Henry?

4. Are the entries into the fire-filled house by Henry (note the name), the Doctor, and the young brakeman like that of Henry Fleming in "The Veteran"? Discuss.

5. Does the term "a thing" imply anything after

the laboratory scene? Do you think it will be related to the title? Why or why not?

6. Why, in retrospect, was the dropping of the picture "The Signing of the Declaration" mentioned when Henry entered the house to rescue the boy?

IX.

1. Why all the local color just at the point of climax?

2. How could rumors be part of the situation when the people must have been aware of who came out and when?

3. Why are there three cots rather than the expected two?

X.

1. Does the newspaper story of Henry Johnson's story sound plausible? What does it give Crane a chance to include?

2. What import does the couplet have?

3. Why would Bella Farragut announce that she had been engaged to Henry?

XI.

1. Why should the suggestion of Henry's being better off dead be put first in the mouth of a judge?

2. Do you think obedience to one's conscience can

really be "a blunder of virtues," as the Judge put it?

3. Was the Judge heartless? Do we have analogous situations for decision, or is this merely an isolated, imaginary instance?

4. Do you think this is a hard decision, assuming, as we must, that the Judge's description of Henry's future state is true? Would the Hippocratic oath enter in as well as Henry's saving of Jimmie?

XII.

1. What is apparent from Henry's answers to the Doctor?

2. At what did Alek Williams scream? and the other Williamses?

XIII.

1. What are Alek's reasons for seeming to turn down the good income he has from the Doctor for taking care of Henry?

2. Is Alek really trying to get that extra dollar more, do you think? Give reasons for your answer.

3. What does the Judge have to do with what Alek gets for boarding Henry?

XIV.

1. The chapter marks a return to the barbershop where Henry Johnson was earlier noted in his color-

ful suit and accessories. Why should a barbershop be chosen for both occasions?

2. Is it important that a majority opinion is established here? Why or why not?

3. Do you think it is coincidence that a railroad brakeman saved Henry and a railroad engineer is now holding "the Doctor should have let him die"?

XV.

1. Why should a fellow deacon give Alek Williams a wide berth? Do you think Crane might have had the Levite in the story of the Good Samaritan in mind? Could it be invoked here?

2. What accounts for Alek's gay mood and what for the change as he approached his home?

3. What do the actions of the Williamses suggest about their relationship to Henry?

4. Why did Alek finally open the door and enter Henry's room, do you suppose?

XVI.

1. Why would Henry be prowling about, looking into windows?

2. Do you think Henry could be as hideous as he is made out to be?

3. Why is Henry never actually described?

XVII.

1. Why does Henry seem so rational on his visit to the Farraguts?

2. Why does the author never call Henry by name (except for the judge doing so in Chapter XII) but always "the monster" or "the thing"?

3. Whose is the more rational behavior here? Discuss.

XVIII.

1. Do you think the chief of police is sympathetic?

2. What does he mean, referring to the people throwing rocks at Henry, "Of course nobody really wanted to hit him, but you know how a crowd gets"?

3. Since people refer to Henry as a devil, a deacon avoids his caretaker, and the father of the horrified children wants to have the Doctor arrested, would you think there is any parallel to witchhunting?

XIX.

1. Is Martha Goodwin's name apropos?

2. Can you identify the Martha type in neighborhoods? Explain.

3. Among her dreams of early days one was "of the face of a man." Why is her "dead passion" described thus?

4. Is it plausible that Kate Goodwin and Carrie

Dungen transfer the scaring property to Dr. Trescott himself?

XX.

1. Is it understandable that Jimmie doesn't recognize his rescuer at first?

2. What is the significance of his going up and saying; "Hello, Henry" when he has done so?

3. Does the children's game seem natural to them? Would they come to it of their own accord and/or through influence from their parents? Discuss.

XXI.

1. Why are the Doctor's talks with Jimmie and Mr. Winter put into the same chapter?

2. Do you think Mr. Winter felt he was getting the best of the Doctor? Why or why not? Of what importance is this?

XXII.

1. Kate and Carrie are types, clearly. Is Martha also? Give reasons for your answer.

2. If Sadie Winter has been going to school regularly, how do you account for her continued illness? Discuss.

3. How does Martha's remark regarding "everybody" being afraid of Henry parallel her comment

on Sadie Winter? What kind of outlook do you think she has? What does this say about the outlook of the others?

4. What is the nature and extent of Henry's monsterdom? Weigh all factors carefully in your answer.

XXIII.

1. Do you think the men who came to see the Doctor were sincere in their intentions? in their saying they admired him for what he had done? Is it true, as they say, that the fault lies with the women?

2. Is there any evidence that Henry went about freely in the town? How was he dressed when he was in the yard?

Research Question

In Hawthorne's short story "The Minister's Black Veil" that piece of crepe became a bar between the clergyman and his parishioners. Is Henry's case analogous?

3. Why not a public institution for Henry? Would this not be a fair enough compromise? Discuss.

4. Why does the Judge say nothing? Is his office of any significance in his first suggestion to the Doctor and now in his silence?

XXIV.

1. What is the role of Mrs. Trescott in all this? To what extent was she central throughout? Why did we

not hear anything of her from her hysteria at the fire until now?

2. Of what importance are guests for tea compared to Trescott's loss in practice?

3. Why would Mrs. Twelve still come, but the Judge's wife not?

4. Why is the redness of the sun on the windows mentioned twice?

5. Critics have sometimes pointed to this chapter as a flaw because it is an anticlimax. Do you agree? Discuss.

6. Had you thought Martha would play a stronger role subsequently? What then is her function in the story?

solace, crimpling, scintillant, cortege, obeisance, equipage, pantomimic, homage, adamantine, mausoleum, palpable, craven, coign, querulously

Research Question

Read the story "The Carriage Lamps" and figure out from it the changes that must have taken place in the Trescott household since the occurrence of "The Monster." Does even the tone of the story suggest anything?

"The Bride Comes to Yellow Sky"

I.

1. Why should the newlyweds be such an object of merriment and snobbery to the porter? to other passengers?

2. How would you characterize their language? their taste? their experience?

3. Why were they relieved to be out of the diner?

4. What, to summarize the specific intent of the first three questions, is Crane trying to get at regarding the couple?

5. What kind of status did he have in Yellow Sky? Why is his name revealed just now?

6. Why did he feel uneasy, almost guilty?

7. Why were they both so self-conscious as they alit at Yellow Sky?

mesquit, coquetry, sardonic, equanimity, commensurately, heinous, plainscraft, fatuously

II.

1. Why is the easy quiet of late afternoon in a saloon built up so carefully?

2. Have we encountered before the kind of danger evidently represented by Scratchy Wilson?

3. What else do we learn by way of exposition about Scratchy? about Jack Potter?

4. When the three men heard shots, "It instantly removed a bond from the men . . ." What does this mean?

5. Why are only the bartender and drummer behind the bar?

drummer, cleft, peremptory

III.

1. Of what importance can it possibly be that Scratchy's shirt was made by Jewish women on New York's East Side? likewise that his were New England boots?

2. Would you say Scratchy was a good shot? How did his drunkenness affect his accuracy? Does that seem realistic? why or why not?

3. Why would Scratchy shoot up the windows of his closest friend?

4. Why did he fume when he got no notice from Jack Potter's house?

imperturbable, fusilladed, immobility

IV.

1. Do you think Scratchy meant to kill Potter in cold blood?

2. Why do images of the pullman go through the consciousness of Potter?

3. Why did Scratchy believe Potter and not even frisk him?

4. Is the notion of being married the entire key to Potter's success in Scratchy's saying "it's off"?

5. Is Scratchy sentimental? What do funnel shaped tracks have to do with anything?

6. Does Scratchy's drunkenness finally show in his turning his back on Potter?

7. Note the relatively strong use of polysyllabic words, for Crane, that is. Why would he do so here,

where his own English seems almost to ridicule the speech of Potter and his bride?

Research Question

Search your recollection for other such deathly confrontations we have encountered in Crane. Is there any consistency in the reasons for their often being settled short of death?

"The Blue Hotel"

At a Nebraska local stop, Scully meets all possible guests for his hotel, this time a Swede, an Easterner and a cowboy. The Swede is evidently scared from reading dime novels about the West. Scully family reminiscences and whiskey seem to reverse the Swede into an aggressive role. During a post-dinner card game, the Swede accuses Johnson of cheating, beats him in a fair fight, moves to the town saloon and there in picking on a professional gambler is stabbed to death. Johnson had cheated, says the Easterner later, and holds that he and four others are as much responsible for the murder as the gambler.

I.

1. The prairies have many extremely clear days in which the sky, as someone once said, is like a great inverted blue bowl. What would such a day do for Pat Scully's aesthetic masterpiece as the trains swung in or through? Would the contour of the country contribute anything to the hotel's visual prominence?

2. How did the Swede differ from the other two new arrivals?

3. When the Swede looks as though he is frightened and remarks about the dangers of Western towns, what are we meant to suspect?

II.

1. What new oddness (for here) did the Swede manifest?

2. How does Scully the elder serve as demonstration that the Swede may well be crazy, and that his behavior is certainly unusual?

3. When Scully's son protests his innocence, why do the others not support him until asked?

4. Why does Scully get so nearly frantic?

III.

1. Did Scully really resemble a murderer? Is the point of view shifted here?

2. Do you think all those improvements Scully mentioned were imminent in Fort Romper? Explain.

3. Why did the Swede hesitate to drink and then drink with hatred for the old man?

IV.

1. Do you think the Easterner's theory about the Swede is plausible? The theory suggests once more

a relationship between life and art that Crane has spoken of before; where and how?

2. What had happened to the Swede in the interim, would you judge?

3. Is Johnnie's summary of the Swede's behavior right?

V.

1. Do you think that the Easterner's diagnosis may still be true and that the Swede is now playing an opposite role as the one to assure survival?

2. Do the Swede's three words continue to hold out the possibility of a dime novel? What would be artistic equivalents today?

3. What accounts for Scully's change of attitude?

VI.

1. As the Easterner sees the preparations for the fight, does he now feel that art has become life, in the sense that all are now going through a ritual called for by the circumstances? Why is he so nervous? Discuss.

2. The cowboy and Scully are obviously for Johnnie. What is the Easterner's attitude here? Is he too playing a role?

3. Why do the girls cry shame on all three of the others? Is Johnnie perhaps the women's boy and so turns out a disappointment to his father?

VII.

1. Why did Scully refuse to take any money from the Swede?

2. Would it really be unfair for one of them to challenge the Swede, especially when he taunted Bill? or was Bill afraid?

3. Are the imaginary fistic antics of the two perhaps too elaborate to be convincing?

VIII.

1. What does the cosmic second paragraph here have to do with the story that has thus far unfolded?

2. Do you think it was the whiskey that changed the Swede or had he pretended terror earlier? Which is the real Swede?

3. Is there a conventional role into which the professional gambler also fits, dime novel and/or community?

4. Ironically, the Swede unwittingly now lays hands on a real cheater, a professional one, and gets murdered. Why a knife rather than fists?

5. Why did the merchant and district attorney evaporate so quickly? Was the gambler as cowardly?

6. How does the line atop the cash register apply to the Swede? to any of the other purchasers?

IX.

1. In the conversation between the Easterner and the cowboy with whom do we tend to side?

2. Are we to accept the Easterner's judgment as final? What about the earlier terrified Swede and his reversal? What about Scully doing right by his guests, and running the fight fairly? Did Johnnie cheat in a game for fun deliberately to assure a go against the Swede? Would not the girls also be involved in the guilt? Are not the other three men at the gambler's table also culpable? Does the theory finally lead to a one-thing-follows-another principle, so that no one is really to blame, an utter naturalistic view (see that second paragraph of chapter XIII)?

3. Is this surprise ending characteristic of Crane? What details suggest that the Easterner is withholding knowledge? Could these be as readily applicable to some other cause, the weather for instance? Or has the Swede already caught Johnnie cheating in the game before dinner, as when he says to him, "Oh, you know what I mean all right" and the father later calls his son "you young divil," feeling sure Johnnie *has* done something? Or are they all finally indirect victims of the dime novel?

4. Why should the story be called "The Blue Hotel"?

5. How do cowardice and courage enter here in the overall, beyond the usual Crane situation of catastrophe or near such? Does this story also demon-

strate the import of environmental pressures as conditioning influence?

Research Question

Recheck all the instances we have come across in which people in the aggregate have been more cruel than as individuals. Compare Crane and Twain's *The Adventures of Huckleberry Finn* from this standpoint.

opulence, profligate, celerity, effulgence, ruminatively, morosely, bacchanal, leonine

Research Questions

In "Death and the Child," a story out of Crane's covering of the campaign for Greek independence, Peza is a Greek correspondent being shown the front who wants to fight for Greece. He is finally offered the chance and flees, though he had not been afraid during the inspection. Is this another exploration of who gets cowardly when? Discuss.

Toward the end of his short life Crane wrote a final series of war stories.

(1) Take the actions of the fighting men in "The Price of the Harness" and "An Episode of War" and compare to some of those depicted by Ernie Pyle, correspondent who covered World War II, in attitude toward participants and descriptive elements.

(2) Compare the Crane men's behavior with that celebrated in a famous "classic," Elbert Hubbard's *The Message To Garcia*, looking up also Crane's letter to Hubbard on the subject.

(3) Can you sense the difficulty in "The Up-

turned Face"? Do you think the problem is made too explicit because of mention, dashes, and length? Discuss.

Two late Whilomville stories deal with Jimmie Trescott, one of them actually bringing together old Henry Fleming and young Jimmie. Compare "Lynx-Hunting" and "The Carriage-Lamps" with stories about grown-ups that just miss the tragic by a hairsbreadth ("Five White Mice," "Horses-One Dash," and "The Bride Comes to Yellow Sky").

Melvin Schoberlin, editor of *The Sullivan Sketches*, has noted Crane's characteristic use of color already in these early sketches. Find examples functionally essential to some of the sketches and compare their use with such in any later Crane work(s). Compare also the "camera angle" in "Killing His Bear" and *The Red Badge of Courage*.

Compare the outlook and work of the painter protagonist of *The Third Violet* with Crane's own impression of language. To what extent do you find them comparable despite the difference in medium?

Is George's drinking in *George's Mother* compulsive in itself or is it compelled by other considerations or both? Does your answer make any difference to the novel? Does the novel belong in the same category of outlook as its predecessors, *Maggie* and *The Red Badge*?

Critical Potpourri
on Crane

Yet Crane was plainly a preface to naturalism, with his gaunt "soldiers of fortune," Bowery toughs, cadavers, wars, morbid catastrophes, and mood of *laissez faire*. Action and atavism flavored his stories of lean, intrepid men, marching wits, muscle, and courage in pre-Adamic conflicts; and he ushered in a whole literature, devoted to cruelty, adventure, wayfaring, lechery, and "strong, silent men" who thirst for money, "life in the raw," or women, and run amok down the peaceful avenues of society.

Harry Hartwick in *The Foreground of American Fiction*. New York: American Book Co., 1934, 44.

In *Maggie* the mind is not entered; the crisis is presented only by swift and ironic reconstruction of environment and surrounding characters. By sheer sincerity the story rises to a conviction in which Howells could detect the "fatal necessity which dominates Greek tragedy" and the simplicity of effect of true art. Naive unprecedented candor of theme, its sense of fate, and its directness in dealing with sordid material. Its lack of sensuality makes it seem almost pale today, but the fire in its unsold paper-backed copies smoldered until the acclaim accorded to his next work made a new edition possible. With that re-publication (1896), modern American fiction was born.

Robert E. Spiller in *Literary History of the United States*. Vol. II, New York: The Macmillan Company, 1948, 1022.

Maggie, divided into 19 chapters or episodes, is a panorama of impressionistic vignettes, disconnected scenes that reel off with much the same jerky, nervous effect that early motion pictures convey. Not logic but mood defines the relationship between images and episodes. Moods of romantic sentiment, illusion or hope collapse in contradictory moods of futility, dis-illusionment or despair.

R. W. Stallman in "Stephen Crane's Primrose Path," *New Republic*, Vol. 133 (September 19, 1955), 17.

Crane's ruling passion was curiosity. Eager for sen-sations, he was always ready to risk his own existence in order to know "how it felt," and he was hyper-sensitive,—neither the tremor of a butterfly's wing nor the quivering of a leaf ever escaped him. How slight were the subjects of many of his sketches,—a man meets a snake on a mountain path, a bear falls off a precipice entangled in a tent, some soldiers hesi-tate to throw the earth on the upturned face of a dead comrade, but, slight as they were, these events as-sumed, because of the acuteness of his own sensibility,

—at once, in the reader's mind,—a prodigious importance. Crane's touch, moreover, was invariably light and swift. To use one of his own phrases, he wrote with the "pace of youth."

Van Wyck Brooks in *The Confident Years*. New York: E.P. Dutton & Co. Inc., 1952, 142.

If we were to seek a geometrical shape to picture the significant form of *The Red Badge*, it would not be the circle, the L, or the straight line of oscillation between selfishness and salvation, but the equilateral triangle. Its three points are instinct, ideals, and circumstance. Henry Fleming runs along the side like a squirrel in a track. Ideals take him along one side until circumstance confronts him with danger. Then instinct takes over and he dashes down the third side in a panic. The panic abates somewhat as he approaches the angle of ideals, and as he turns the corner (continuing his flight) he busily rationalizes to accommodate those ideals of duty and trust that recur, again and again, to harass him. Then he runs on to the line of circumstance, and he moves again toward instinct. He is always controlled on one line, along which he is both drawn and impelled by the other two forces. If this triangle is thought of as a piece of bright glass whirling in a cosmic kaleidoscope, we have an image of Crane's naturalistic and vividly impressioned Reality.

Charles Walcutt in *American Literary Naturalism: A Divided Stream*. Minneapolis: University of Minnesota, 1956, 82.

From this moment, reached on the thirtieth page, the drama races through another hundred and sixty pages to the end of the book, and to read those pages is in itself an experience of breathless, lambent, detonating life. So brilliant and detached are the images evoked that, like illuminated bodies actually seen, they leave their fever-bright phantasms floating before the brain. You may shut the book, but you still see the battle-flags "jerked about madly in the smoke," or sinking with "dying gestures of despair," the men "dropping here and there like bundles"; the captain shot dead with "an astonished and sorrowful look as if he thought some friend had done him an ill turn"; and the litter of corpses, "twisted in fantastic contortions," as if "they had fallen from some great height, dumped out upon the ground from the sky." The book is full of sensuous impressions that leap out from the picture: of gestures, attitudes, grimaces, that flash into portentous definition, like faces from the climbing clouds of nightmare. It leaves the imagination bounded with a "dense wall of smoke, furiously slit and slashed by the knife-like fire from the rifles." It leaves, in short, such indelible traces as are left by the actual experience of war.

George Wyndham "A Remarkable Book," *New Review*, XIV (January 1896), 35-36.

The Black Riders is the best place to study the element of revolt in the poetry of the Nineties. Most of the young men who rebelled against tradition were satisfied to make a complete break with their past and their society and find various replacements for the lost ideologies. Crane rebelled, and he made clear what he was rebelling against. Repressed by the opinions and conventions of his society, he sought an individual expression in which to voice his protest. His expression in the form he adopted is his true contribution to American poetry. His themes and his attitudes can be duplicated in the poetry of the Nineties: Crane's portrait of God, his indictment of man, and even his romantic retreat were echoed in *Ballads of Revolt* written by J. S. Fletcher in 1897. But Fletcher used traditional forms while Crane found a new freedom, breaking completely with the English tradition that ruled such a large section of his own scene.

Carlin T. Kindilien in *American Poetry in the Eighteen Nineties.* Providence: Brown University Press, 1956, 159-160.

Crane's special contribution to the development of fiction is his concentrated use of the metaphoric and symbolic aspects of language to advance the action and to extend the implications of his themes. This significant technical resource is used in his stories to reinforce the more conventional structure of plot which he conserved from his "clever Rudyard-Kipling style." The second advantage inhering in his prose style is that Crane's metaphoric imagination can operate under much freer conditions in fiction than those his poems allowed. Variety of situation, the presentation of character, and the invention of incident make necessary a salutary concreteness in the fiction writer's conception of his materials. His language will, if successful, reflect this concreteness; and if, like Crane, he has a primarily sensuous response to experience, his metaphors will combine passion with immediacy of perception. These are qualities, however, which in many of his poems Crane would seem to have gone to some lengths to deny himself. Yet the limitations in his verse are present partly because of his use there of a narrative technique.

Daniel G. Hoffman in *The Poetry of Stephen Crane*. New York: Columbia University Press, 1957, 221-222.

"The Open Boat" is to my mind, beyond all question, the crown of all his work. It has all the stark power of the earlier stories, with a new element of restraint; the color is as full and strong as ever, fuller and stronger indeed; but those chromatic splashes that at times deafen and confuse in "The Red Badge," those images that astonish rather than enlighten, are disciplined and controlled."

H.G. Wells. "Stephen Crane from an English Standpoint," *North American Review*, CLXXI (August, 1900), 237.

"The Blue Hotel," although it has a different emphasis from "The Open Boat," is similar in subject matter and artistic technique. Here too we find Nature at war or seemingly so, with man, ethical motivation along with deterministic behavior, the element of chance, the attempt at understanding, and the ultimate refusal to guarantee anything about what a man "owes" his destiny to. There is a greater focus here, however, on man's pretentiousness and vaingloriousness. Heroism is decidedly absent. The story counterpoises the theme of man's arrogance in even existing, let alone in pretending to moral behavior and to understanding on this "space-lost bulb," and the idea that one must withal act morally and try to interpret his experience.

Stanley B. Greenfield in "The Unmistakable Stephen Crane", *PMLA*, LXXIII (December 1958), 566.

He began with the somber-jocular, sable, fantastic prose of the "Sullivan County Sketches" and the jagged, colored, awkward, brilliant *Maggie*. *Maggie* he probably revised much barbarousness out of before anyone except brothers and friends saw it, and he abandoned deliberately the method of the sketches —though fantasy, and fantasy in the quality of the prose, remained intermittently an element in his work to the end. A movement towards fluidity increases in *The Red Badge* and the "Baby Sketches" he was writing at the same time and produces a Crane norm: flexible, swift, abrupt, and nervous—swift, but with an unexampled capacity for stasis also. Color is high, but we observe the blank absence of the orotund, the moulded, which is Crane's most powerful response to the prose tradition he declined to inherit. In the fusion

of the impassive and the intense peculiar to this author, he kept on drawing the rein. "Horses—One
Dash" and "The Five White Mice" lead to the supple
majesty of "The Open Boat," a second norm. *The
Monster*, much more closed, circumstantial, "normal"
in feeling and syntax, is a third. Then he opened his
style again back towards the second norm in the
great Western stories, "The Bride Comes to Yellow
Sky" and "The Blue Hotel," and thereafter (for his
two years) he used the second and third styles at will,
sometimes in combination, and the third usually re-
laxed as his health failed but peculiarly tense and as-
tonishing in "The Kicking Twelfth." In certain late
work also, notably in "The Clan of No Name," a
development toward complexity of structure is evident, which death broke off. Nevertheless we may
speak of "Crane's style" so long as we have these
variations in mind, and my point is that it differs
radically both from the tradition of English prose and
from its modifications in American prose.

John Berryman in *Stephen Crane*. New York: William Sloane
Associates Inc., 1950, 284.

Let it be stated that the mistress of this boy's mind
was fear. His search in aesthetic was governed by
terror as that of tamer men governed by the desire of
women. "Maggie" had represented the terror of an
environment tinged by social judgment. In all the
Mexican and Texan sketches appears, as in "The Red
Badge of Courage," a vision of man's identity faced

by its end, by incomprehensible death. One gets the solid courage of the marshall of Yellow Sky who shoves annihilation from him by a simple statement; the rogue of "A Man and Some Others" dies easily because he is bound by contract to defend his flock. In the true story, "Horses" and the fanciful "Five White Mice," one sees Crane himself, recording his own pulse before a shadow which he refused to kneel and worship. He could be afraid, and afraid with all the quivering imagination of an artist—here stood the great death and here, mentally or in flesh, stood he. But his recording of the state is never more than civilly sympathetic.

Thomas Beer in *Stephen Crane*. Garden City: Garden City Publishing Co. Inc., 1927, 117-118.

I have spoken of Crane as the first American writer. The claim is not new, though I do not know who made it first. I dare say I did because I must certainly have been one of the first to think it. It remains perhaps a little controversial. But all American writers who preceded him had their eyes on Europe. They may have aped Anglicism in their writings, like the Concord group; or, like Mark Twain—or even if you like, O. Henry—they were chronic protesters against Europeanism. At any rate, the Old World preoccupied them.

There was nothing of this about Crane.

Ford Madox Ford in *Portraits from Life*. New York: Houghton Mifflin Company, 1937, 35.

Selective Bibliography
on Crane and His Works

1. Bibliography

Beebe, Maurice, and Gullason, Thomas A. "Criticism of Stephen Crane; A Selected Checklist with an Index to Studies of Separate Works," *Modern Fiction Studies*, V (Autumn, 1959), 282-291.

   This issue is a Crane number, with articles by Peter Buitenhuis, James B. Colvert, James T. Cox, Robert F. Glockner, Thomas A. Gullason, James Hafley, Hugh N. MacLean, Eric Solomon, and R. W. Stallman.

Hoffman, Daniel G. *The Poetry of Stephen Crane*. New York: Columbia University Press, 1957.

   Lists many unpublished items, and publishes some for the first time.

All the standard biographies include solid selective bibliographies.

Spiller, Robert E., *et al. Literary History of the United States.* New York: The Macmillan Company, 1946, Vol. III, 458-461; also,

   Bibliography Supplement, Edited by Richard M. Ludwig, 1959, 100-101.

Stolper, B.J.R. *Stephen Crane: A List of His Writings and Articles About Him.* Newark, N.J.: Newark Public Library, 1930.

Williams, Ames W., and Starrett, Vincent. *Stephen Crane: A Bibliography.* Glendale, California: John Valentine, Publ. 1948.

2. Text

A number of paperbacks of careful editorship continue to appear. For listing see Walter Harding's annual compilation of paperback reprints edited for the American Literature Section of the Modern Language Association.

Crane, Stephen. *Men, Women and Boats*. Edited with an Introduction by Vincent Starrett. New York: Boni and Liveright, 1921.

Crane, Stephen. *Maggie, Together with George's Mother and The Blue Hotel*. Introduction by Henry Hazlitt. New York: Alfred A. Knopf, 1931.

Follett, Wilson (ed). *The Collected Poems of Stephen Crane*. New York: Alfred A. Knopf, 1930.

Follett, Wilson (ed). *The Work of Stephen Crane*. 12 vols. New York: Alfred A. Knopf, 1925-27.

   The separate volumes have introductions by Carl Van Doren, Amy Lowell, Willa Cather, H.L. Mencken, Robert H. Davis, Joseph Hergesheimer, etc.

Hoffman, Daniel G. "Stephen Crane's New Jersey Ghosts: Two Newly-Recovered Sketches," *Proceedings of a New Jersey Historical Society*, LXXI (October, 1953), 239-253.

Lettis, Richard; McDonnell, Robert F; and Morris, William E. (eds). *The Red Badge of Courage: Text and Criticism*. New York: Harcourt, Brace, and Company, 1960.

   Reprints in an Appendix the text of those passages in Crane's final manuscript (see Stallman below), but not in the first American edition. The criticism consists mainly of substantial excerpts from 26 articles.

Schoberlin, Melvin (ed). *The Sullivan County Sketches of Stephen Crane*. Syracuse, N.Y.: Syracuse University Press, 1949.

Stallman, Robert W. (ed). *Stephen Crane, An Omnibus*. New York: Alfred A. Knopf, 1952.

   Includes two novels, short stories, poems, newspaper pieces, and letters. Especially valuable for the edition of *The Red Badge of Courage* from manuscript, for the history of *Maggie*, and for newspaper accounts, including Crane's own, of the event fictionalized in "The Open Boat."

Stallman, R.W., and Gilkes, Lillian (eds). *Stephen Crane: Letters*. New York: New York University Press, 1960.

   Excellently edited with a comprehensive continuity. It is not the fault of the editors that most of the correspondence concerns the rigors of his daily existence. Crane had little reading and so even less criticism. But the desperation, anything but Thoreauvianly quiet, is there in all its acuteness.

Stallman, Robert W. "Stephen Crane: Some New Stories," *Bulletin of the New York Public Library*, LX:9 (September, 1956), 455-462, and LX:10 (October, 1956), 477-486.

Stallman, R.W. "Stephen Crane's Revisions of *Maggie: A Girl of the Streets, American Literature*, XXVI (January, 1955), 528-536.

Van Doren, Carl (ed). *Stephen Crane: Twenty Stories*. New York: Alfred A. Knopf, 1940.

3. Biography

Much new material, especially letters, suggest the necessity for a new biography. Berryman does not displace Beer, though he corrects some informational aspects. The Stallman Gilkes edition of the letters corrects both, but in a sense the value of both biographers lies primarily in the spirit and method of treating Crane's life and work in their interrelationship.

Beer, Thomas. *Stephen Crane: A Study in American Letter*. Introduction by Joseph Conrad. New York: Alfred A. Knopf, 1923.

   (The prefaced memoir by Conrad is a fine tribute to a friend and to their relationship)

Berryman, John. *Stephen Crane*. New York: William Sloan Associates, Inc., 1950.

Cather, Willa. "When I Knew Stephen Crane," *Prairie Schooner*, XXIII (Fall, 1949), 231-237.

Conrad, Joseph. "Stephen Crane: A Note Without Dates," *Bookman*, L (February, 1920), 529-531.

Ford, Ford Madox. *Portraits from Life*. Boston: Houghton Mifflin Company, 1937, 21-37.

Franchere, Ruth. *Stephen Crane: The Story of an American Writer*. New York: Thomas Y. Crowell Company, 1961.

   A biography for young readers in story form.

Garland, Hamlin. "Stephen Crane as I Knew Him," *Yale Review* n.s. III (April, 1914), 494-506.

Gilkes, Lillian. *Cora Crane: A Biography of Mrs. Stephen Crane*. Bloomington: Indiana University Press, 1960.

Linson, Corwin K. *My Stephen Crane*. Edited with an introduction by Edwin H. Cady. Syracuse: Syracuse University Press, 1958.

O'Donnell, Thomas F. "John B. Van Petten: Stephen Crane's History Teacher," *American Literature*, XXVI (January 1956), 196-202.

   A personal source for actions of men under fire.

Osborn, Scott C. "The Rivalry-Chivalry of Richard Harding Davis and Stephen Crane," *American Literature*, XXVII (March, 1956), 50-61.

Prat, Lyndon Upson. "The Formal Education of Stephen Crane," *American Literature*, X (January 1939), 460-471.

Williams, Ames W. "Stephen Crane, War Correspondent," *New Colophon*, I (April, 1948), 113-123.

4. Criticism

Selection of criticism covering a writer's entire work does injustice to the necessary filling out of the critical picture while concentrating on limited indicative directions.

Ahnebrink, Lars. *The Beginnings of Naturalism in American Fiction*. New York: Russell & Russell, 1961.

Brennan, Joseph X. "The Imagery and Art of *George's Mother*," *CLA Journal*, IV (December, 1960), 106-115.

Colvert, James B. "The Origins of Stephen Crane's Literary Credo," *University of Texas Studies in English*, XXXIV (1955), 179-188.

Cox, James T. "Stephen Crane as Symbolic Naturalist: An Analysis of 'The Blue Hotel,'" *Modern Fiction Studies*, III (Summer, 1957), 147-158.

Day, Cyrus. "Stephen Crane and the Ten-foot Dinghy," *Boston University Studies in English*, III (Winter, 1957), 193-213.
    Factual background of "The Open Boat."

Elconin, V.A. "Stephen Crane at Asbury Park," *American Literature*, XX (May, 1948), 275-289.

Friedman, Norman. "Criticism and the Novel: Hardy, Hemingway, Crane, Wolfe, Conrad," *Antioch Review*, XVIII (Fall, 1958), 343-370.

Garnett, Edward. "Stephen Crane: An Appreciation." *Friday Nights*. New York: Alfred A. Knopf, 1922, 203-213.

Geismar, Maxwell. *Rebels and Ancestors: The American Novel, 1890-1915*. Boston: Houghton, Mifflin & Company, 1953.

Gordon, Caroline. "Stephen Crane," *Accent*, IX (Spring 1949), 153-157.
    Penetrating study of point of view, using "The Open Boat" as illustration.

Gullason, Thomas A. "The Jamesian Motif in Stephen Crane's Last Novels," *The Personalist*, XLII (Winter, 1961), 77-84.

Gullason, Thomas A. "The Symbolic Unity of 'The Monster'" *Modern Language Notes*, XXV (December, 1960), 663-668.

Hagemann, E.R. "Crane's 'Real' War in His Short Stories," *American Quarterly*, VIII (Winter, 1956), 356-367.
    Succinct, penetrating analysis of Crane's concept of the individual soldier.

Hartwick, Harry. *The Foreground of American Fiction*. New York: American Book Company, 1934, 21-44.

Hoffman, Daniel G. *The Poetry of Stephen Crane*. New York: Columbia University Press, 1957.

Hough, Robert L. "Crane and Goethe: A Forgotten Relationship," *Nineteenth Century Fiction*, XVII (September, 1962), 135-148.

Howells, W.D. "New York Low Life in Fiction," *New York World*, July 26, 1896.

Josephson, Matthew. *Portrait of the Artist as American*. New York: Harcourt, Brace & Co., 1930, 232-264.

Kindilien, Carlin T. *American Poetry in the Eighteen Nineties*. Providence: Brown University Press, 1956, 155-161.

Klotz, Marvin. "Stephen Crane: Tragedian or Comedian," *University of Kansas City Review*, XXVII (March, 1961), 170-174.
> Analysis of "The Blue Hotel."

Kwiat, Joseph J. "The Newspaper Experience: Crane, Norris, and Dreiser," *Nineteenth Century Fiction*, VIII (September, 1953), 99-117.

Kwiat, Joseph J. "Stephen Crane and Painting," *American Quarterly*, IV (Winter, 1952), 331-338.

Leaver, Florence. "Isolation in the Work of Stephen Crane," *South Atlantic Quarterly*, LXI (Autumn, 1962), 521-532.

Liebling, A.J. "The Dollars Damned Him," *New Yorker*, XXXVII (August, 1961), 48-72.

Marcos, Mordecai, and Marcos, Erin. "Animal Imagery in *The Red Badge of Courage*," *Modern Language Notes*, LXXIV (February, 1959), 108-111.

Munson, Gorham B. *Style and Form in American Prose*. New York: Doubleday, Doran & Co. Inc., 1929, 159-170.
> Detailed analysis of "The Open Boat."

Nye, Russell B. "Stephen Crane as Social Critic," *Modern Quarterly*, XI (Summer, 1940), 48-54.

O'Donnell, Thomas F. "An Analysis of the Poetry of Stephen Crane," Masters Thesis, Syracuse University, 1947.

Randel, William. "The Cook in 'The Open Boat,'" *American Literature*, XXXIV (November, 1962), 405-411.

Ross, Lillian. *Picture*. New York: Rinehart & Company, 1952.
> The filming of *The Red Badge* from first notice to edited version.

Shroeder, John W. "Stephen Crane Embattled," *University of Kansas City Review*, XVII (Winter, 1950), 119-129.

Solomon, M. "Stephen Crane: A Critical Study," *Masses and Mainstream*, IX (January, 1956), 25-42, (March, 1956), 31-47.
> Finds Crane's work less negativistic than is sometimes thought.

Spiller, Robert E., *et al*. *Literary History of the United States*. New York: The Macmillan Company, 1946. vol. II, 1020-1026.

Stallman, R. W. "Stephen Crane's Primrose Path," *New Republic*, CXXXIII (September 19, 1955), 17-18.
> Analysis of *Maggie*

Starrett, Vincent. "Stephen Crane: An Estimate," *Sewanee Review*, XXVIII (July, 1920), 405-413.

Stein, William B. "New Testament Inversions in Crane's *Maggie*," *Modern Language Notes*, LXXIII (April, 1958), 268-272.

Stein, William B. "Stephen Crane's *Homo Absurdus*," *Bucknell Review*, VIII (May, 1959), 168-188.

Stevenson, John W. "The Literary Reputation of Stephen Crane," *South Atlantic Quarterly*, LI (April, 1952), 286-300.

Sutton, Walter. 'Pity and Fear in "The Blue Hotel," ' *American Quarterly*, IV (Spring, 1952), 73-78.

Walcutt, Charles Child. *American Literary Naturalism, A Divided Stream*. Minneapolis: University of Minnesota Press, 1956.

Webster, H. T. "Wilbur Hinman's *Corporal Si Klegg* and Stephen Crane's *The Red Badge of Courage*," *American Literature*, XI (May 1939), 285-293.

Wells, H. G. "Stephen Crane from an English Standpoint," *North American Review*, CLXXI (August, 1900), 233-242.

Westbrook, May. "Stephen Crane: The Pattern of Affirmation," *Nineteenth Century Fiction*, XIV (December, 1959), 219-229.

Wogan, Claudia C. "Crane's Use of Color in 'The Red Badge of Courage,' " *Modern Fiction Studies*, VI (Summer, 1960), 168-172.